the Homo Deuce

The Godless Globalist Great Reset Plan Exposed In Their Own Words

CLAY CLARK

"A crafty exposure of Schwab & Harari's psychological nudity." - Clay Clark

ISBN: 979-8-9864278-1-2

Copyright 2022 by Clay Clark

Clay Clark Publishing

Published by Thrive Publishing
3920 West 91st Street South
Tulsa, OK 74132

Printed in the United States of America

"Once it was 100% clear to me that "The Great Reset" was being implemented by Klaus Schwab, I committed myself to doing whatever I could do to help save this nation for my five kids, for my family, for my country, for my clients, and for myself."

- CLAY CLARK

Visit TimeToFreeAmerica.com/TheHomoDeuce to watch the video clips referenced throughout this book.

WHY WAS THIS BOOK WRITTEN?

This book was written to provide you with a POWERFUL TOOL to help you wake up your family and friends to "The Great Reset" and "Fourth Industrial Revolution" agenda that is being forced upon us using the actual words of Yuval Noah Harari and Klaus Schwab who are two of the most influential men leading "The Great Reset." Klaus Schwab is the founder of the World Economic Forum and Yuval Noah Harari is a historian, a best-selling author who has sold over 40 million copies of his books, a professor in the Department of History at the Hebrew University of Jerusalem and a man praised by Barack Obama, Mark Zuckerberg, Bill Gates, Stanford, Harvard, MIT, TEDTalks, New York Times, James Corden, the vast majority of the Silicon Valley tech tycoons and the mainstream media. On Yuval Noah Harari's website (https://www.ynharari.com/) his slogan "History began when humans invented gods and will end when humans become gods" is prominently and proudly presented. Who Am I?

My name is Clay Clark. I'm the co-founder of five incredible kids, I've been married to the same incredible woman (Vanessa Clark) for 21 years and I'm a man who has been blessed to achieve tremendous business success by the world's standards. I'm the organizer, the emcee

Visit TimeToFreeAmerica.com/TheHomoDeuce to watch the video clips referenced throughout this book.

and host of the General Flynn ReAwaken America Tour (www.TimeToFreeAmerica.com), the former "U.S. SBA Entrepreneur of the Year" for the State of Oklahoma.

I'm the founder of several multi-million dollar companies, the host of the Thrivetime Show podcast, which has been number one overall on the iTunes business podcast charts 6 times. I've been a member of the Forbes Business Coach Council, I have been an Amazon best-selling author, I host of the Thrivetime Show podcast and throughout my career I've founded / co-founded several multi-million dollar businesses including:

- www.DJConnection.com
- www.EpicPhotos.com
- www.EITRLounge.com
- www.MakeYourLifeEpic.com
- Party Perfect (Which was purchased by Party Pro Rentals)
- www.TipTopK9.com

Visit TimeToFreeAmerica.com/TheHomoDeuce to watch the video clips referenced throughout this book.

WHAT DO I DO FOR A LIVING?

Like many of you reading this, I grew up with limited financial means and a lack of financial resources, so at the age of 14-15 I started my quest to become a millionaire before the age of 30. In route to achieving my goals I won a bunch of business awards and was asked to speak for many big-time companies including Hewlett Packard, Farmers Insurance, Maytag University, Valspar Paint, EXP Realty, UPS, etc. Many attendees at these speaking events, conferences began asking me to teach them my proven processes, success strategies and my best-practice business growth systems and so that is what I did. Thus, beginning around 2006 I began taking on business growth consulting clients and the success that my clients achieved was EPIC!!! To date I have documented over 2,000 + clients success stories and case studies at: www.thrivetimeshow.com/testimonials/ So, when asked what I do for a living I tell people that I teach people how to start and grow businesses, but I also grow businesses myself. Why? Because I enjoy it and God has blessed me with a skill set to grow businesses. So if you are out there and you want to attend the world's highest rated and most reviewed small business workshops that I host or you want to learn how I can help you to start and grow your own successful business check out: www.ThrivetimeShow.com.

Visit TimeToFreeAmerica.com/TheHomoDeuce to watch the video clips referenced throughout this book.

IF I'M A BUSINESS GUY WHO GROWS BUSINESSES WHY AM I THE GUY HOSTING THE REAWAKEN AMERICA TOUR AND WRITING THIS BOOK?

After exhaustively researching the issues related to COVID-19 and right before the COVID-19 lockdowns hit all of America, it occurred to be that the following items were TRUE:

> »**The Models That Predicted That 2.2 Million Americans Would Die from COVID-19 Were False and Funded by Bill Gates**

> *- See the Supporting Documentation - https://timetof-reeamerica.com/the-models/#scroll-content*

> »**The PCR Tests, the COVID-19 Tests and the Polymerase Chain Reaction Tests That Were Being Used to Test for COVID-19 Were Being Misused and Falsely Calibrated to Inflate the Number of Positive COVID-19 Cases**

Visit TimeToFreeAmerica.com/TheHomoDeuce to watch the video clips referenced throughout this book.

- Watch the Inventor of the PCR Tests (Karry Mullis) Explain - https://rumble.com/v1chwrl-karry-mullis-why-did-the-inventor-of-the-pcr-tests-call-dr.-fauci-a-liar.html

....

»The System and Method for Testing for COVID-19 Was Patented In 2015 - See the Patent

- https://pubchem.ncbi.nlm.nih.gov/patent/US-2020279585-A1

....

»The Treatment Protocols Being Used to Treat COVID-19 Patients Including Remdesivir (Which Is a Drug Patented by George Soros and China In Conjunction with Gilead Labs) and Midazolam Were Killing People - See the Supporting Documentation

- https://timetofreeamerica.com/follow-the-money/#scroll-content & https://timetofreeamerica.com/covid-19-deadliness/#scroll-content

NOTE: Remdesivir has been shown to cause renal failure

NOTE: Midazolam is a breath suppressant

....

»The Effective and Affordable Treatments for COVID-19 Were Being Withheld from the American People Including: Budesonide, Ivermectin and Hydroxycholoquine - See the Supporting Documentation

- https://timetofreeamerica.com/treatments/#scroll-content

....

»Klaus Schwab Has Been Working On What He Calls the Fourth Industrial Revolution / The Great Reset Since 1971:

See Klaus Schwab Explain, "It Dates Back to 1971. It's Now 600 Highly Educated People Located Around the World Particularly In Geneva Where Our Headquarters Is. The Fourth Industrial Revolution Is Very Disturbing Progress for Many People."

- WATCH: https://rumble.com/v1x9sgw-klaus-schwab-the-history-of-the-world-economic-forum-it-dates-back-to-1971..html

See Joe Biden Deliver the Keynote Address at the World Economic Forum On "Mastering the Fourth Industrial Revolution In 2016"

- WATCH: https://rumble.com/v1itvsx-joe-biden-why-did-biden.html

See Prince Charles Deliver the Keynote Address the 2020 World Economic Forum Annual Meeting In Davos, Switzerland

- WATCH - https://www.youtube.com/watch?v=bcwuluYL9bw

Read Klaus Schwab's Book Titled, COVID-19: The Great Reset

- https://www.amazon.com/COVID-19-Great-Reset-Klaus-Schwab/dp/2940631123

SO HOW DID YOUR RESEARCH LEAD TO STARTING THE REAWAKEN AMERICA TOUR?

Once it was 100% clear to me that "The Great Reset" was being implemented by Klaus Schwab I committed myself to doing whatever I could to help save this nation for my five kids, for my family, for my country, for my clients and for myself. Thus, I sued the Mayor of Tulsa to keep the city of Tulsa open during the lockdowns, I turned my building into a town hall meeting center / church during the lockdowns, I brought in Sean Feucht and others to host praise and worship events when we were told that churches should be closed and the people should not gather, I dramatically changed the format of my podcast to explain to our listeners what COVID-19 was truly all about and why it was killing their businesses, The urgency of these matters led to a sleepless, sweaty night—I was attacked with visions of what I was supposed to do. I felt like God was calling me to host an event with General Flynn where we would share the truth about election fraud, medical fraud, religious fraud, mainstream media fraud and monetary freedom, but at the end of the day it had to be about leading people back to God. So I called General Flynn

Visit TimeToFreeAmerica.com/TheHomoDeuce to watch the video clips referenced throughout this book.

and told him that I felt that we were supposed to team up to host an event that would share the truth about the fraud on our country and the solution, and he immediately said, "I know, but it has to happen through the church!" Thus, less than 60 days later I hosted the first ReOpen America / ReAwaken America Tour event in Tulsa, Oklahoma where 5,500 people were in attendance and millions were watching online featuring fearless patriots and followers of Christ like General Flynn, Mike Lindell, Sidney Powell, etc.

»**To get the full story, you can watch the documentary for free at:**

www.TimeToFreeAmerica.com

WHY ME?

I feel called by God to help ReAwaken America and to lead millions back to Christ and that is what I am going to do. People that know me know that I am super aggressive, very organized and I have a relentless work ethic, but I'm not that impressive. I'm just trying to use 100% of my time, my talents and my treasure to lead people to Christ and to expose TheGreat Reset / Fourth Industrial Revolution / Transhumanism agenda. However, please never put your faith in me or any of my wonderful friends who are working tirelessly to help save America (General Flynn, Kash Patel, Doctor Eric Nepute, Doctor Sherri Tenpenny, Eric Trump,

Visit TimeToFreeAmerica.com/TheHomoDeuce to watch the video clips referenced throughout this book.

Mike Lindell, Pastor Leon Benjamin, Pastor Mark Burns, Pastor Greg Locke, Doctor Stella Immanuel, Jim Breuer, etc.). Remember that we are just flawed people that do not deserve salvation, but who are committed to doing what we can to help save this nation while sharing the Gospel and the good news of the eternal salvation that can only be received after you accept Jesus Christ as your Lord and Savior and the begin to repent of your sins and begin to earnestly seek to follow his ways and his teachings found within his Word of God known as "The Bible."

»**"That if thou shalt confess with thy mouth the Lord Jesus, and shalt believe in thine heart that God hath raised him from the dead, thou shalt be saved. For with the heart man believeth unto righteousness; and with the mouth confession is made unto salvation."**

- Romans 10:9-10

Visit TimeToFreeAmerica.com/TheHomoDeuce to watch the video clips referenced throughout this book.

13

HOW TO READ
THIS BOOK:

It should take you approximately 1 hour to read this book. As you read through this book, wrestle with the content. Take notes, look up everything I am referencing, and visit: www. TimeToFreeAmerica.com/TheHomoDeuce to find a digital copy of this book so that you can click on all of the hyperlinks, website references and citations found within this book. You can also find the entire Great Reset timeline explained in a linear format today at: www.TimeToFreeAmerica. com/Revelation. Click on the hyperlinks, the patents and the proof I am presenting to prove every claim that I am making throughout the pages of this book. After you have invested the 1 hour of time total needed to understand the nefarious Great Reset transhumanism agenda, I encourage you to invest the time needed to read the scriptures (The 100% irrefutable word of God) referenced throughout the pages of this book as well because we must remember what Ephesians Chapter 6 verses 12-13 reads, "12 For we wrestle not against flesh and blood, but against principalities, against powers, against the rulers of the darkness of this world, against spiritual wickedness in high places 13 Wherefore take unto you the whole armor of God, that ye may be able to withstand in the evil day, and having done all, to stand."

Visit TimeToFreeAmerica.com/TheHomoDeuce to watch the video clips referenced throughout this book.

"Humans are hackable animals."

- YUVAL NOAH HARARI

*Visit TimeToFreeAmerica.com/TheHomoDeuce to watch
the video clips referenced throughout this book.*

"Humans are hackable animals."

"You will own nothing
and you will be happy."

- KLAUS SCHWAB

Visit TimeToFreeAmerica.com/TheHomoDeuce to watch the video clips referenced throughout this book.

CHAPTER 1

WHO ARE THE TWO KEY INDIVIDUALS LEADING "THE GREAT RESET" AGENDA?

Klaus Schwab and Yuval Noah Hararri are the two key leaders of creating, narrating and implementing both "The Great Reset" agenda and "The Great Narrative" Agenda.

WHO IS KLAUS SCHWAB?

Klaus Schwab is the author of *COVID-19 / The Great Reset*, and *The Great Narrative*. Klaus Schwab is the founder of the World Economic Forum (The World Economic Forum's logo is '666'). Yuval Noah Harari is an Israeli lead advisor for Klaus Schwab. Klaus Schwab was born March 30, 1938 in Ravensburg, Germany. Schwab's father ran the Escher Wyss factory which was celebrated as the "National Socialist Model Company" by Adolf Hitler.

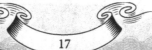

Visit TimeToFreeAmerica.com/TheHomoDeuce to watch the video clips referenced throughout this book.

WHO IS YUVAL NOAH HARARI?

Yuval Noah Harari is an Israeli-born World Economic Forum member and a lead advisor for Klaus Schwab.

Yuval Noah Harari is an openly gay best-selling author who has sold over 40 million copies of his books. He abstains from eating meat and is celebrated by Barack Obama, Mark Zuckerberg, and Bill Gates. Yuval Noah Harari is praised by the New York Times, Stanford, TED, MIT, Silicon Valley and TimesTalks. Yuval is a Hebrew first name which means "father of music," stream, brook, or tributary. In the Hebrew Bible, Yuval (also Jubal) was the son of Lamech and Adah and a descendant of Cain who is referenced in Genesis 4:20-21. To learn more about the mindset of Yuval Noah Harari read 2nd Thessalonians Chapter 2. Yuval Noah Harari is an Israeli public thought leader, an intellectual, a historian, an outspoken proponent of the transhumanism agenda and a professor in the Department of History at the Hebrew University of Jerusalem.

Visit TimeToFreeAmerica.com/TheHomoDeuce to watch the video clips referenced throughout this book.

Visit TimeToFreeAmerica.com/TheHomoDeuce to watch the video clips referenced throughout this book.

> »**Watch The Great Reset Transhumanism-Nano-Tech Agenda Explained In Their Own Words:**

> *https://rumble.com/vvqqpn-the-great-reset-vs-the-great-re-awakening-the-transhumanism-nano-tech-agenda.html*

> »**Watch Yuval Noah Harari & Klaus Schwab Advisor Describe "Humans Are Hackable Animals" while declaring "Free Will Is Over"**

> *https://rumble.com/vxg5xv-yuval-noah-harari-klaus-schwab-advisor-humans-are-hackable-animals-and-free.html*

Visit TimeToFreeAmerica.com/TheHomoDeuce to watch the video clips referenced throughout this book.

"Humans have invented God.
Humans have invented Heaven and Hell.
Humans have invented free will."

- YUVAL NOAH HARARI

*Visit TimeToFreeAmerica.com/TheHomoDeuce to watch
the video clips referenced throughout this book.*

CHAPTER 2:

What Other Names Are Used When Describing the "The Great Reset?"

The "Great Reset" is also known as: COVID-19, The Great Reset, The Fourth Industrial Revolution, Transhumanism, the New World Order Event 201 and Agenda 2030.

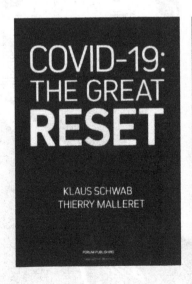 

Visit *TimeToFreeAmerica.com/TheHomoDeuce to watch the video clips referenced throughout this book.*

"600 Highly-Educated People Located Around the World... that's the forum."

- KLAUS SCHWAB

Visit *TimeToFreeAmerica.com/TheHomoDeuce* to watch the video clips referenced throughout this book.

CHAPTER 3:

What Has Yuval Noah Harari Actually Said About the Future?

WHAT DOES YUVAL NOAH HARARI BELIEVE?

On the homepage of Yuval Noah Harari's website (www.YNHarari.com) Yuval Noah Harari writes, "History began when humans invented gods and will end when humans become gods."

> »Klaus Schwab Lead Advisor Praised by Obama, Zuckerberg & Gates, Yuval Noah Harari stated, "COVID Is Critical Because This Is What Convinces People to Accept to Legitimize Total Biometric Surveillance. If We Want to Stop This Epidemic, We Need to Monitor What's Happening Under Their Skin."

- WATCH - https://rumble.com/v1xa4fg-yuval-noah-harari-covid-is-critical-because-this-is-what-convinces.html

»Why Did Dr. Fauci Team Up with TJ Jakes to Push the COVID-19 mRNA-Modifying-Nano-Technology-Filled Vaccines?

- WATCH - *https://twitter.com/BishopJakes/status/135230 7633043206146?s=20&t=WHO6B1hbwtjFQI8GDH35UQ*

» Klaus Schwab Lead Advisor Praised by Obama, Zuckerberg & Gates, Yuval Noah Harari stated, "The New Powers That We Are Gaining Now, the Powers of Biotechnology and Artificial Intelligence Are Going to Transform Us Into Gods"

- WATCH - *https://rumble.com/v1x8z3o-yuval-noah-harari-the-new-powers-that-we-are-gaining-now-the-powers-of.html*

» Klaus Schwab Lead Advisor Praised by Obama, Zuckerberg & Gates, Yuval Noah Harari stated, "Nationalism Is a Barrier for Cooperation On the International Level. The President of the U.S. (Trump) Said That There Is a Contradiction Between Nationalism and Globalism and That People Should Choose Nationalism and Reject Globalism. But, I Think This a Mistake."

- WATCH - *https://rumble.com/v1xh9sq-yuval-noah-harari-trump-nationalism-is-a-barrier-for-cooperation.html*

Visit TimeToFreeAmerica.com/TheHomoDeuce to watch the video clips referenced throughout this book.

»Klaus Schwab Lead Advisor Praised by Obama, Zuckerberg & Gates, Yuval Noah Harari stated, "A Change In the U.S. Administration (Removing Trump) Will Make It Easier Because the Current Administration Is Being a Negative Force Even Undermining the World Health Organization and Attempts At Global Cooperation."

- WATCH - https://rumble.com/v1xhb3k-yuval-noah-harari-trump-a-chance-in-the-u.s.-administration-removing-trump-.html

» Klaus Schwab Lead Advisor Praised by Obama, Zuckerberg & Gates, Yuval Noah Harari stated, "Trump Is Destroying the U.S. Alliance System All Over the World. He's Destroying the Greatest Achievement of the U.S. Foreign Policy for Decades to Build This Global Alliance System."

- WATCH - https://rumble.com/v1xhaok-yuval-noah-harari-trump-trump-is-destroying-the-u.s.-alliance-system-all-ov.html

» Klaus Schwab Lead Advisor Praised by Obama, Zuckerberg & Gates, Yuval Noah Harari stated, "COVID-19 Should Lead to the Establishment of a Global Healthcare System."

- WATCH - https://rumble.com/v1287u7-yuval-noah-harari-covid-19-should-lead-to-the-establishment-of-a-global-hea.html

Why Did Dr. Fauci Team Up with TJ Jakes to Push the COVID-19 mRNA-Modifying-Nano-Technology-Filled Vaccines?WATCH - https://rumble.com/v1287u7-yuval-noah-harari-covid-19-should-lead-to-the-establishment-of-a-global-hea.html

Visit TimeToFreeAmerica.com/TheHomoDeuce to watch the video clips referenced throughout this book.

»The Klaus Schwab Lead Advisor Praised by Obama, Zuckerberg & Gates, Yuval Noah Harari stated, "COVID Accelerates the Process of Digitalization, It Legitimizes the Deployment of Mass Surveillance and It Makes Surveillance Go Under Your Skin."

WATCH - https://rumble.com/v1r2zpy-yuval-noah-harari-covid-legitimizes-the-deployment-of-mass.html

»The Klaus Schwab Lead Advisor Praised by Obama, Zuckerberg & Gates, Yuval Noah Harari stated, "Jesus Never Claimed to Be God, He Was Basically This Hippy Guru Who Wanted to Reform Judaism. Jesus Did Not Think He Was Yahweh. Decades After He Is Dead, People Say This Rabbi Who Had a Small Following Was Actually the God That Created the Whole of the Universe."

WATCH - https://rumble.com/v1w6i6c-yuval-noah-harari-jesus-never-claimed-to-be-god.html

»The Klaus Schwab Lead Advisor Praised by Obama, Zuckerberg & Gates, Yuval Noah Harari stated, "In Order to Solve the Climate Crisis We Will Need to Give Up Alot of Our Most Cherished Needs."

WATCH - https://rumble.com/v1o8b8p-yuval-noah-harari-in-order-to-solve-the-climate-crisis.html

KLAUS SCHWAB
"You will own nothing and be happy."

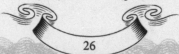

Visit TimeToFreeAmerica.com/TheHomoDeuce to watch the video clips referenced throughout this book.

»The Klaus Schwab Lead Advisor Praised by Obama, Zuckerberg & Gates, Yuval Noah Harari stated, "The World Cannot Go On Relying On the U.S. And Waiting Every 4 Years to See Who the U.S. Elects This Time." and "There Is a Chance That the Next Presidential Election Would Be the Last Election In U.S. History."

WATCH - https://rumble.com/v1qqqm8-yuval-noah-harari-the-world-cannot-go-on-relying-on-the-u.s..html

»The Klaus Schwab Lead Advisor Praised by Obama, Zuckerberg & Gates, Yuval Noah Harari stated, "If People Are Less Required In the Workplace The Big Question Will Be What to Do with All the People. It's Netflix Mushrooms or Computer Games."

WATCH - https://rumble.com/v1oabew-yuval-noah-harari-.html

»The Klaus Schwab Lead Advisor Praised by Obama, Zuckerberg & Gates, Yuval Noah Harari stated, "We Are One of the Last Generations of Homo Sapiens."

WATCH - https://rumble.com/v1ko8cr-yuval-noah-harari-we-are-one-of-the-last-generations-of-homo-sapiens..html

»The Klaus Schwab Lead Advisor Praised by Obama, Zuckerberg & Gates, Yuval Noah Harari stated, "We Will Never Reach Perfection. We Just Need to Be Better Than Humans. If We Switch to Self-Driving Vehicles We Saved 700,000 Lives Every Year."

Visit TimeToFreeAmerica.com/TheHomoDeuce to watch the video clips referenced throughout this book.

WATCH - https://rumble.com/v109fb2-self-driving-cars-yuval-noah-harari-.html

»**The Klaus Schwab Lead Advisor Praised by Obama, Zuckerberg & Gates, Yuval Noah Harari stated, "Democracies Might Be Less Efficient Than Dictatorships and Meaningless?"**

WATCH - https://rumble.com/v1cpri7-yuval-noah-harari-democracies-might-be-less-efficient-than-dictatorships-an.html

»**The Klaus Schwab Lead Advisor Praised by Obama, Zuckerberg & Gates, Yuval Noah Harari stated, "Humans' Feelings Are Highest Authority. You Don't Appeal to God or the Bible."**

WATCH - https://rumble.com/v1474pj-yuval-noah-harari-humans-feelings-are-highest-authority.-you-dont-appeal-to.html

YUVAL NOAH HARARI

"Humans are now hackable animals. The whole idea that humans have this soul or spirit, and they have free will, and nobody knows what's happening inside me, so whatever I choose whether in the election or whether in the supermarket, f. "

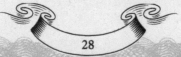

Visit TimeToFreeAmerica.com/TheHomoDeuce to watch the video clips referenced throughout this book.

»**The Klaus Schwab Lead Advisor Praised by Obama, Zuckerberg & Gates, Yuval Noah Harari stated, "The Big Battle Will Be Between Privacy & Health, People Will Give Up Privacy."**

WATCH - https://rumble.com/v18trwa-yuval-noah-harari-the-big-battle-will-be-between-privacy-and-health-people-.html

»**The Klaus Schwab Lead Advisor Praised by Obama, Zuckerberg & Gates, Yuval Noah Harari stated, "We Are Now Basically the Gods of Planet Earth."**

WATCH - https://rumble.com/v11bb6c-yuval-noah-harari-wef-lead-advisor-we-are-now-basically-the-gods-of-planet-.html

»**The Klaus Schwab Lead Advisor Praised by Obama, Zuckerberg & Gates, Yuval Noah Harari stated, "For the First Time In History, It Is Possible to Completely Eliminate Privacy."**

WATCH - https://rumble.com/v1uyjgk-canadi-an-prime-minister-justin-trudeau-.html

»**The Klaus Schwab Lead Advisor Praised by Obama, Zuckerberg & Gates, Yuval Noah Harari stated, "Christianity Is a Human Creation."**

WATCH - https://rumble.com/v126wft-yuval-no-ah-harari-christianity-is-human-creation.html

Visit TimeToFreeAmerica.com/TheHomoDeuce to watch
the video clips referenced throughout this book.

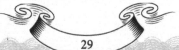

»**The Klaus Schwab Lead Advisor Praised by Obama, Zuckerberg & Gates, Yuval Noah Harari stated, "Earth Will Be Dominated by (Non-Organic) Entities."**

WATCH - https://rumble.com/v1a009l-yuval-noah-harari-earth-will-be-dominated-by-non-organic-entities.html

»**The Klaus Schwab Lead Advisor Praised by Obama, Zuckerberg & Gates, Yuval Noah Harari stated, "People Will Lose Control of Their Lives. The Meaning of Life Is Changing."**

WATCH - https://rumble.com/v1a00kj-yuval-noah-harari-people-will-lose-control-of-their-lives.-the-meaning-of-l.html

»**The Klaus Schwab Lead Advisor Praised by Obama, Zuckerberg & Gates, Yuval Noah Harari stated, "Total Surveillance Regime The System Monitors Everybody All the Time."**

WATCH - https://rumble.com/v1d4htd-yuval-noah-harari-total-surveillance-regime-the-system-monitors-everybody-a.html

»**The Klaus Schwab Lead Advisor Praised by Obama, Zuckerberg & Gates, Yuval Noah Harari stated, "What Does It Mean to Live Life Where Decisions Are Managed by Outside Systems?"**

- WATCH - https://rumble.com/v1141t9-yuval-noah-harari-what-does-it-mean-to-live-life-where-decisions-are-manage.html

Visit TimeToFreeAmerica.com/TheHomoDeuce to watch the video clips referenced throughout this book.

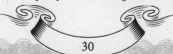

»The Klaus Schwab Lead Advisor Praised by Obama, Zuckerberg & Gates, Yuval Noah Harari stated, "Dictatorships Will Be More Efficient Than Democracies. Democracy Defeated Fascism & Communism Because Democracy Was Better At Processing Data and Making Decisions."

WATCH - *https://rumble.com/v1n4mbq-yuval-noah-harari-dictatorships-will-be-more-efficient.html*

»The Klaus Schwab Lead Advisor Praised by Obama, Zuckerberg & Gates, Yuval Noah Harari stated, "My Job Is to Build a Bridge Between the Scientific Community & Public."

WATCH - *https://rumble.com/v109ez8-yuval-noah-harari-my-job-is-to-build-a-bridge-between-the-scientific-commun.html*

»The Klaus Schwab Lead Advisor Praised by Obama, Zuckerberg & Gates, Yuval Noah Harari stated, "5G Will Allow the Detection Before You Even Feel the Symptoms."

WATCH - *https://rumble.com/v10pfvx-world-economic-forum-5g-will-allow-the-detection-before-you-even-feel-the-s.html*

»The Klaus Schwab Lead Advisor Praised by Obama, Zuckerberg & Gates, Yuval Noah Harari stated, "In the 21st Century We'll Have New Data-Ist Religion. Authority Is Algorithms."

Visit TimeToFreeAmerica.com/TheHomoDeuce to watch the video clips referenced throughout this book.

WATCH - https://rumble.com/v1a04x4-yuval-noah-harari-in-21st-century-well-have-new-data-ist-religion.-authorit.html

»**The Klaus Schwab Lead Advisor Praised by Obama, Zuckerberg & Gates, Yuval Noah Harari stated "What we've seen so far is corporations and governments collecting data about where we go, who we meet, what movies we watch. The next phase is the surveillance going under our skin."**

WATCH - https://rumble.com/v10cxoz-yuval-noah-harari-hilter-and-stalin-would-be-nothing-compared-to-the-combin.html

»**The Klaus Schwab Lead Advisor Praised by Obama, Zuckerberg & Gates, Yuval Noah Harari stated, "There Is No God In the Universe and No Human Rights."**

WATCH - https://rumble.com/vymns1-yuval-noah-harari-there-is-no-god-in-the-universe-and-no-human-rights.html

»**The Klaus Schwab Lead Advisor Praised by Obama, Zuckerberg & Gates, Yuval Noah Harari stated, "Authority & Power Will Shift Away from Humans to Computers & Most Humans Will Become Economically Useless & Politically Powerless."**

WATCH - https://rumble.com/v1h671f-yuval-noah-harari-why-did-yuval-noah-harari-say.html

Visit TimeToFreeAmerica.com/TheHomoDeuce to watch the video clips referenced throughout this book.

»**The Klaus Schwab Lead Advisor Praised by Obama, Zuckerberg & Gates, Yuval Noah Harari stated, "Christianity Has No True Essence. We Will See the Emergence of New Religions."**

WATCH - https://rumble.com/v128a6n-yuval-noah-harari-christianity-has-no-true-essence.-we-will-see-the-emergen.html

»**The Klaus Schwab Lead Advisor Praised by Obama, Zuckerberg & Gates, Yuval Noah Harari stated, "Poor People Will Not Be Able to Heat Their Houses and They Will Suffer."**

WATCH - https://rumble.com/v186zdo-yuval-noah-harari-poor-people-will-not-be-able-to-heat-their-houses-and-the.html

»**The Klaus Schwab Lead Advisor Praised by Obama, Zuckerberg & Gates, Yuval Noah Harari stated, "Direct Brain-Computer Interfaces, Adding a Second Inorganic Immune System Made Out of Millions of Tiny Nano Robots"**

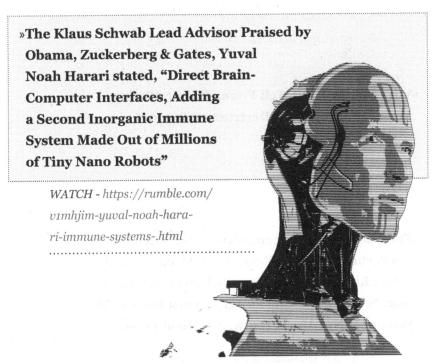

WATCH - https://rumble.com/v1mhjim-yuval-noah-harari-immune-systems-.html

Visit TimeToFreeAmerica.com/TheHomoDeuce to watch the video clips referenced throughout this book.

»The Klaus Schwab Lead Advisor Praised by Obama, Zuckerberg & Gates, Yuval Noah Harari stated, "People Will Literally Be Part of a Network, All of the Bodies, All the Brains Will Be Connected to a Network and You Won't Be Able to Survive If You're Disconnected from the Net. Because Your Own Immune System Depends On Constantly Being Connected to the Network." "

WATCH - https://rumble.com/v1c9dt1-yuval-noah-harari-your-immune-systems-will-be-connected-to-net.html

»The Klaus Schwab Lead Advisor Praised by Obama, Zuckerberg & Gates, Yuval Noah Harari stated, "COVID Was the Moment When Surveillance Started Going Under the Skin."

WATCH - https://rumble.com/v19irhx-yuval-noah-harari-covid-was-the-moment-when-surveillance-started-going-unde.html

»Why Did the POPE Tell Young People "Eating Meat Is Part of a Self-Destructive Trend?"

WATCH - https://rumble.com/v1f7zyd-climate-emergency-why-does-the-pope-tell.html

»The Klaus Schwab Lead Advisor Praised by Obama, Zuckerberg & Gates, Yuval Noah Harari stated, "The Chief Value of Science Is Power. Science Is Mainly About Gaining Power Against the World. Science Is Not About Truth, It's About Power."

Visit TimeToFreeAmerica.com/TheHomoDeuce to watch the video clips referenced throughout this book.

WATCH - https://rumble.com/v1qt2f2-yuval-noah-ha-rari-the-chief-value-of-science-is-power..html

» **Why Did the Prosperity Preaching Pastor Creflo Dollar Support Pro-Abortion Stacey Abrams?**

WATCH - https://rumble.com/v1qufgc-woke-pas-tors-why-is-the-prosperity-preaching-pastor-creflo-dollars.html

» **The Klaus Schwab Lead Advisor Praised by Obama, Zuckerberg & Gates, Yuval Noah Harari stated, "You Have a Small ELITE That Pushes Things. Probably for the Elite It Will Work. When the Flood Comes the Scientists Will Build a Noah's Ark for the ELITE Leaving the Rest to Drown."**

WATCH - https://rumble.com/v1qgr04-yuval-noah-ha-rari-you-have-a-small-elite-that-pushes-things..html

» **The Klaus Schwab Lead Advisor Praised by Obama, Zuckerberg & Gates, Yuval Noah Harari stated, "If We Invest 2% of the Global GDP This Should Be Enough to Stop Catastrophic Climate Change."**

WATCH - https://rumble.com/v1qgpg4-yuval-no-ah-harari-if-we-invest-2-of-the-global.html

KLAUS SCHWAB
"The World Economic Forum Is the Connecting Organization. We Need An Approach Where We Integrate All ACTORS."

Visit TimeToFreeAmerica.com/TheHomoDeuce to watch the video clips referenced throughout this book.

»**The Klaus Schwab Lead Advisor Praised by Obama, Zuckerberg & Gates, Yuval Noah Harari stated, "Computers Will Have an Exquisitely Fine Tuned Understanding of How We Feel. We Will Become Very Intolerant of Self-Centered Humans Who Don't Understand How We Feel."**

WATCH - https://rumble.com/v1q2hlg-yuval-noah-harari-computers-will-have-an-exquisitely.html

»**The Klaus Schwab Lead Advisor Praised by Obama, Zuckerberg & Gates, Yuval Noah Harari stated, "More and More People Will Become Irrelevant and Useless. Maybe If the Powerful Are Nice They Will Give You Something Like Universal Basic Income."**

WATCH - https://rumble.com/v1pzjhf-yuval-noah-harari-more-and-more-people-will-become-irrelevant-and-useless..html

»**The Klaus Schwab Lead Advisor Praised by Obama, Zuckerberg & Gates, Yuval Noah Harari stated, "To Follow In the Footstep of Jesus Doesn't Mean to Say I Believe That Jesus Christ Is the Savior. So You Believe In Jesus Christ, So What?"**

WATCH - https://rumble.com/v1pzjrz-yuval-noah-harari-to-follow-in-the-footstep-of-jesus-doesnt-mean-to-say-i-b.html

Visit TimeToFreeAmerica.com/TheHomoDeuce to watch the video clips referenced throughout this book.

»The Klaus Schwab Lead Advisor Praised by Obama, Zuckerberg & Gates, Yuval Noah Harari stated, "The Hitlers of the 21st Century with Tools Like A.I. and Bioengineering, They Will Have the Ability to Reengineer the Human Body and the Mind."

WATCH - https://rumble.com/v1pi3uz-yuval-noah-harari-the-hitlers-of-the-21st-century.html

»Klaus Schwab | "We Have Now a Window of Opportunity to Create This Global Reset, Using Technologies of the Fourth Industrial Revolution, Artificial Intelligence, the Internet of Things, the Capabilities That We Have with Genetic Editing."

WATCH - https://rumble.com/v1w5y30-klaus-schwab-.html

»The Klaus Schwab Lead Advisor Praised by Obama, Zuckerberg & Gates, Yuval Noah Harari stated, "You Don't Need Any Religion or Any Government to Have Morality Because Morality Is Not About Obeying a Certain Set of Laws Because Morality Is About Suffering."

WATCH - https://rumble.com/v1phypd-yuval-noah-harari-you-dont-need-any-religion-or-any-government.html

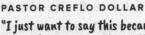

PASTOR CREFLO DOLLAR

"I just want to say this because I want to see how it sounds. Governor Stacey Abrams just walked in. [Applause] So you already know what to do, right? How many of you have already done it? [Applause] Wow. It's big time. Make it happen. Do what you got to do."

Visit TimeToFreeAmerica.com/TheHomoDeuce to watch the video clips referenced throughout this book.

»The Klaus Schwab Lead Advisor Praised by Obama, Zuckerberg & Gates, Yuval Noah Harari stated, "What Is the Role of Our Bodies? Is the Point to Release Our Mind or Our Soul from This to Exist In an Immaterial Realm? This Theological Battle from 2,000 Years ago Is Now Becoming a Real Battle."

WATCH - https://rumble.com/v1phlxp-yuval-noah-harari-what-is-the-role-of-our-bodies.html

»The Klaus Schwab Lead Advisor Praised by Obama, Zuckerberg & Gates, Yuval Noah Harari stated, "We May See the Emergence of a New Massive Class of Useless People."

WATCH - https://rumble.com/v1d7ipd-yuval-noah-harari-we-may-see-the-emergence-of-a-new-massive-class-of-useles.html

»The Klaus Schwab Lead Advisor Praised by Obama, Zuckerberg & Gates, Yuval Noah Harari stated, "Authority Will Shift Away from Humans. Most Humans Will Become USELESS."

WATCH - https://rumble.com/v1876d5-yuval-noah-harari-authority-will-shift-away-from-humans.-most-humans-will-b.html

»The Klaus Schwab Lead Advisor Praised by Obama, Zuckerberg & Gates, Yuval Noah Harari stated, "Humans Will Become...Politically POWERLESS."

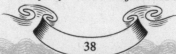

Visit TimeToFreeAmerica.com/TheHomoDeuce to watch the video clips referenced throughout this book.

WATCH - https://rumble.com/v161wpp-yuval-noah-harari-authority-will-shift-away-from-humans-to-computers.-human.html

»**The Klaus Schwab Lead Advisor Praised by Obama, Zuckerberg & Gates, Yuval Noah Harari stated, "What Do We Do With All of These Useless People? The Masses Even If They Organize Don't Stand Much of a Chance?"**

WATCH - https://rumble.com/v1edslx-yuval-noah-harari-what-do-we-do-with-all-of.html

»**The Klaus Schwab Lead Advisor Praised by Obama, Zuckerberg & Gates, Yuval Noah Harari stated, "This Metaverse Fantasy Is Taking Over Many People and Minds In Silicon Valley and Elsewhere."**

WATCH - https://rumble.com/v1n4miy-yuval-noah-harari-this-metaverse-fantasy-is.html

»**The Klaus Schwab Lead Advisor Praised by Obama, Zuckerberg & Gates, Yuval Noah Harari stated, "Christians Say They Have a Recipe for a Kingdom On Earth. Then They Gain Power...and You Get The Inquisition."**

WATCH - https://rumble.com/v1vhrg2-yuval-noah-harari-christians-say-they-have-a-recipe-for-a-kingdom.html

YUVAL NOAH HARARI
"Jesus Never Claimed to Be God, He Was Basically This Hippy Guru Who Wanted to Reform Judaism. Jesus Did Not Think He Was Yahweh. Decades After He Is Dead, People Say This Rabbi Who Had a Small Following Was Actually God."

Visit TimeToFreeAmerica.com/TheHomoDeuce to watch the video clips referenced throughout this book.

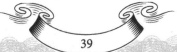

»The Klaus Schwab Lead Advisor Praised by Obama, Zuckerberg & Gates, Yuval Noah Harari stated, "Only a Real Catastrophe Can Shake Humankind and Open the Path to a Real System of Global Governance."

WATCH - https://rumble.com/v1emdt1-yuval-noah-harari-only-a-real-catastrophe-can-shake.html

»The Klaus Schwab Lead Advisor Praised by Obama, Zuckerberg & Gates, Yuval Noah Harari stated, "It's Now Technically Possible to Completely Annihilate Privacy. It's Possible to Follow Everyone All of the Time. You Have Cameras and Microphones and Algorithms and Smartphones."

WATCH - https://rumble.com/v1qgnqq-yuval-noah-harari-its-now-technically-possible-to-completely.html

»The Klaus Schwab Lead Advisor Praised by Obama, Zuckerberg & Gates, Yuval Noah Harari stated, "The U.S. Constitution and the 10 Commandments. Both of These Documents Endorse Slavery."

WATCH - https://rumble.com/v1sbroe-yuval-noah-harari-harari-interviewed-on-the-gray-area-podcast-.html

»The Klaus Schwab Lead Advisor Praised by Obama, Zuckerberg & Gates, Yuval Noah Harari stated, "God Is Dead It Just Takes Awhile to Get Rid of the Body."

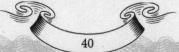

WATCH - https://rumble.com/v10d4oo-yuval-noah-harari-god-is-dead-it-just-takes-awhile-to-get-rid-of-the-body.-.html

»**The Klaus Schwab Lead Advisor Praised by Obama, Zuckerberg & Gates, Yuval Noah Harari stated, "Very Soon It Will Be Possible to Hack Human Beings to Manipulate Emotions."**

WATCH - https://rumble.com/v1dkwyz-yuval-noah-harari-very-it-will-be-possible-to-hack-human-beings-to-manipula.html

»**The Klaus Schwab Lead Advisor Praised by Obama, Zuckerberg & Gates, Yuval Noah Harari stated, "The Earth Will Be Dominated by Entities."**

WATCH - https://rumble.com/v1es3b7-yuval-noah-harari-earth-will-be-dominated-by-entities.html

»**The Klaus Schwab Lead Advisor Praised by Obama, Zuckerberg & Gates, Yuval Noah Harari stated, "Many of the Things I Talk About and People In the West React with Fear, In China the Reaction to Exactly the Same Topics Is Excitement. WOW, We Can Do That!"**

WATCH - https://rumble.com/v1o8jqe-yuval-noah-harari-china-.html

KLAUS SCHWAB

"The CHINESE Model Is a Very Attractive Model for a Quite a Number of Countries."

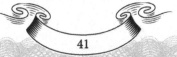

Visit TimeToFreeAmerica.com/TheHomoDeuce to watch the video clips referenced throughout this book.

»The Klaus Schwab Lead Advisor Praised by Obama, Zuckerberg & Gates, Yuval Noah Harari stated, "What Do We Need Humans For? Keep Them Busy with Drugs and Video Games. What to Do With All of These Useless People?"

WATCH - https://rumble.com/v108e5f-yuval-noah-harari-what-do-we-need-humans-for-keep-them-busy-with-drugs-and-.html

»The Klaus Schwab Lead Advisor Praised by Obama, Zuckerberg & Gates, Yuval Noah Harari stated, "Even Somebody Like Stalin, Mao or Hitler Couldn't Figure Out What Is Happening Now. Now We Are Opening Up This Black Box. We Are Beginning to Hack Human Beings."

WATCH - https://rumble.com/v1j78j7-yuval-no-ah-harari-even-somebody-like-stalin.html

»Yuval Noah Harari has stated, "Surveillance Technology Can Be Used to Create the Most Totalitarian Regimes That Ever Existed; Things Far More Totalitarian and Intrusive Than Nazi Germany."

WATCH - https://rumble.com/v1es25t-yuval-no-ah-harari-surveillance-technology-can-be.html

»The Klaus Schwab Lead Advisor Praised by Obama, Zuckerberg & Gates, Yuval Noah Harari stated, "Surveillance Under the Skin" & "Trusting Science is Above Everything Else."

Visit TimeToFreeAmerica.com/TheHomoDeuce to watch the video clips referenced throughout this book.

WATCH - https://rumble.com/vy525f-yuval-noah-harari-sur-veillance-under-the-skin-and-trusting-science-above-ev.html

....

»**The Klaus Schwab Lead Advisor Praised by Obama, Zuckerberg & Gates, Yuval Noah Harari stated, "COVID-19 Could Be A Watershed Moment for Surveillance Under the Skin."**

WATCH - https://rumble.com/v167q41-yuval-noah-harari-covid-19-could-be-a-watershed-moment-for-surveillance-und.html

....

»**The Klaus Schwab Lead Advisor Praised by Obama, Zuckerberg & Gates, Yuval Noah Harari stated, "Stalin Dreamt About Creating a New Man...a New Stalin Could Reengineer a New Body. In the 21st Century a New Stalin Could Really Re-Engineer the Human Body. Anything That Is Possible Is Natural."**

WATCH - https://rumble.com/v1bw2ib-yuval-noah-harari-stalin-dreamt-about-creating-a-new-man.html

....

»**The Klaus Schwab Lead Advisor Praised by Obama, Zuckerberg & Gates, Yuval Noah Harari stated, "The Easiest People to Manipulate Are People That Believe In Free Will"**

WATCH - https://rumble.com/v10do4h-yuval-noah-harari-the-easiest-people-to-manipulate-are-people-that-believe-.html

....

*Visit TimeToFreeAmerica.com/TheHomoDeuce to watch
the video clips referenced throughout this book.*

»Why Did Yuval Noah Harari State, "Decades And Generations After He Is Dead And He Is Not There To Be Able To Object, You Have People Say NO, This Rabbi— This Guru With a Small Following Who Was Eventually Crucified By The Hated Romans, He Was Actually The God That Created The Whole Of The Universe!"

WATCH - *https://rumble.com/v1w6i6c-yuval-noah-harari-jesus-never-claimed-to-be-god.html*

»The Klaus Schwab Lead Advisor Praised by Obama, Zuckerberg & Gates, Yuval Noah Harari stated, "Unless You Invent a Technology to Control Minds, There Isn't a Technological Way to Destroy the Deep Source of Racism." And "We Will Become Gods. We Will Acquire Divine Powers of Creation and Destruction."

WATCH - *https://rumble.com/v1oxwa6-yuval-noah-harari-we-will-become-gods-but-we-will-be-dissatisfied-gods..html*

»The Klaus Schwab Lead Advisor Praised by Obama, Zuckerberg & Gates, Yuval Noah Harari stated, "Humankind Is About the Master New Powers. The Main Product of the Economy In the 21st Century Are Likely to Be Bodies, Brains, and Minds."

WATCH - *https://rumble.com/v1edsot-yuval-noah-harari-the-main-product-of-the-economy-will-be-bodies-brains-and.html*

»The Klaus Schwab Lead Advisor Praised by Obama, Zuckerberg & Gates, Yuval Noah Harari stated, "Fake News Has Been With Us Thousands of Years, Just Think of the Bible."

WATCH - https://rumble.com/v1eio8f-yuval-no-ah-harari-fake-news-has-been-with.html

»The Klaus Schwab Lead Advisor Praised by Obama, Zuckerberg & Gates, Yuval Noah Harari stated, "Humankind Might Split Into Biological Casts and for the First Time In History It Will Be Possible to Translate Economic Inequality Into Biological Inequality."

WATCH - https://rumble.com/v1edsi1-yuval-noah-hara-ri-humankind-might-split-into-biological-casts.html

»The Klaus Schwab Lead Advisor Praised by Obama, Zuckerberg & Gates, Yuval Noah Harari stated, "We Are One of the Last Chapters in the Story of Homo Sapiens."

WATCH - https://rumble.com/v1144c0-yuval-noah-harari-we-are-one-of-the-last-chapters-in-the-story-of-homo-sapi.html

YUVAL NOAH HARARI

"A Change In the U.S. Administration (Removing Trump) Will Make It Easier Because the Current Administration Is Being a Negative Force Even Undermining the World Health Organization and Attempts At Global Cooperation."

Visit TimeToFreeAmerica.com/TheHomoDeuce to watch the video clips referenced throughout this book.

»The Klaus Schwab Lead Advisor Praised by Obama, Zuckerberg & Gates, Yuval Noah Harari stated, "After Thousands of Years, Authority and Power Will Shift Away from Humans to Computers and Most Humans Will Become Economically USELESS and Politically POWERLESS. Creating a New Class of Humans, the USELESS Class."

WATCH - https://rumble.com/v1c8m1n-yuval-noah-harari-.html

»The Klaus Schwab Lead Advisor Praised by Obama, Zuckerberg & Gates, Yuval Noah Harari stated, "The Good Thing About Computer Code Is That It Can Be Corrected Much More Easily (Than Humans)."

WATCH - https://rumble.com/v1gkjw7-yuval-noah-harari-mrna-.html

»The Klaus Schwab Lead Advisor Praised by Obama, Zuckerberg & Gates, Yuval Noah Harari stated, "The Idea That We Punish People for Making Bad Choices That Should Be Out."

WATCH - https://rumble.com/v1c8mhr-yuval-noah-harari-.html

»The Klaus Schwab Lead Advisor Praised by Obama, Zuckerberg & Gates, Yuval Noah Harari stated, "Most People Will Be Willing to Give Up Their Privacy for Better Health Care. Allowing Google, Facebook or the Chinese Government to Constantly Monitor What Is Happening Inside the Human Body."

WATCH - https://rumble.com/v1c8nmv-yuval-noah-harari-.html

Visit TimeToFreeAmerica.com/TheHomoDeuce to watch the video clips referenced throughout this book.

»**Why Did Pastor Rick Warren Endorse the World Economic Forum Agenda & Francis Collins of the National Institutes of Health?**

WATCH - https://rumble.com/vnh2db-why-is-rick-warren-pushing-the-world-economic-forum-agenda-and-endorsing-fr.html

»**The Klaus Schwab Lead Advisor Praised by Obama, Zuckerberg & Gates, Yuval Noah Harari stated, "The Gilgamesh Project Is the Project to Give Humans Eternal Life and to Create Super Humans."**

WATCH - https://rumble.com/v1ezlmj-the-great-reset-what-is-the-gilgamesh-project-singularity-and-the-anthropoc.html

»**The Klaus Schwab Lead Advisor Praised by Obama, Zuckerberg & Gates, Yuval Noah Harari stated, "Human Rights Are Not a Biological Fact." | "There Is No God, No Nations, No Corporations, No Money, No Human Rights and No Justice."**

WATCH - https://rumble.com/v1c8x71-yuval-noah-harari-.html

»**The Klaus Schwab Lead Advisor Praised by Obama, Zuckerberg & Gates, Yuval Noah Harari stated, "You Don't Need Children, You Can Have a Pension Fund. You Don't Need Neighbors, Sisters or Brothers. The State Provides You With Everything."**

WATCH - https://rumble.com/v1ch7et-yuval-noah-harari-.html

Visit TimeToFreeAmerica.com/TheHomoDeuce to watch the video clips referenced throughout this book.

»Why Did Yuval Noah Harari State, "Up Til Now In History, Humans Were So Complicated That, From a Practical Perspective, It Still Made Sense To Believe In Free Will."

https://rumble.com/vxzo99-yuval-noah-harari-yuval-states-jesus-rising-from-the-dead-and-being-the-son.html

»The Klaus Schwab Lead Advisor Praised by Obama, Zuckerberg & Gates, Yuval Noah Harari stated, "We Are In the Process of Turning Ourselves Into Gods and I Mean This In the Most Literal Sense Possible."

WATCH - https://rumble.com/v1c8003-yuval-noah-harari-.html

»The Klaus Schwab Lead Advisor Praised by Obama, Zuckerberg & Gates, Yuval Noah Harari stated, "In One Way We Are Undermining the Ability of Carbon Life to Support Itself and At the Same Time We Are Creating the Conditions for a Completely New Kind of Life. The First Inorganic Life Forms After 4 Billion Years of Evolution."

WATCH - https://rumble.com/v1089s7-yuval-noah-harari-yu-val-shares-an-a.i.-summary-of-his-work.-via-an-a.i.-cre.html

»The Klaus Schwab Lead Advisor Praised by Obama, Zuckerberg & Gates, Yuval Noah Harari stated, "All Religions, All Nations and All Economic Systems Are Based Upon a Fictional Story."

WATCH - https://rumble.com/v1cfcmn-yu-val-noah-harari-money-.html

Visit TimeToFreeAmerica.com/TheHomoDeuce to watch the video clips referenced throughout this book.

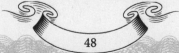

»**The Klaus Schwab Lead Advisor Praised by Obama, Zuckerberg & Gates, Yuval Noah Harari stated, "The Pope Was Very Helpful to Pushing Climate Change."**

WATCH - https://rumble.com/v109hrb-yuval-noah-harari-pope-was-very-helpful-to-push-climate-change-and-jesus-an.html

»**Why Did Andy Stanley Push Pastors to Adhere to the Politically Correct Narrative?**

WATCH - https://www.cnn.com/2022/06/04/us/andy-stanley-evangelicals-book-blake-cec/index.html

»**The Klaus Schwab Lead Advisor Praised by Obama, Zuckerberg & Gates, Yuval Noah Harari stated, "It Is Now Possible for the First Time In History to Build a Total Surveillance Regime. A System In Which Measures All of the Systems All of the Time."**

WATCH - https://rumble.com/v186yul-yuval-noah-harari-total-surveillance-regime.-the-system-monitors-everybody-.html

"(The Great Reset) Is Very Disturbing Progress for Many People and They Just Feel Overwhelmed. And This Creates a Tendency for Nationalism...And That Is One of the Reasons for the Success of TRUMP in the United States."

KLAUS SCHWAB

Visit TimeToFreeAmerica.com/TheHomoDeuce to watch the video clips referenced throughout this book.

»The Klaus Schwab Lead Advisor Praised by Obama, Zuckerberg & Gates, Yuval Noah Harari stated, **"Hilter & Stalin Would Be Nothing Compared to the Combination of AI & Bio-Tech"**

WATCH - https://rumble.com/v1ocxoz-yuval-noah-harari-hilter-and-stalin-would-be-nothing-compared-to-the-combin.html

»The Klaus Schwab Lead Advisor Praised by Obama, Zuckerberg & Gates, Yuval Noah Harari stated, **"It's Not An Extremely Deadly Virus and Look What It Is Doing to the World. So Now Just Try to Think of What Are the Implications of a Much Bigger Problem Like Climate Change. You Can Change Things On a Massive Scale. You Can Lock Down Entire Countries. This May Make Us More Open to Radical Ideas About How to Deal with Climate Change."**

WATCH - https://rumble.com/v1evw21-yuval-noah-harari-its-not-an-extremely-deadly-virus.html

»The Klaus Schwab Lead Advisor Praised by Obama, Zuckerberg & Gates, Yuval Noah Harari stated, **"When Somebody Tells Me How They Are Now Using CRISPR to Overcome Parkinsons, I Think...Hmm, What Would Have Stalin Have Done With That?"**

WATCH - https://rumble.com/v1bwo4j-crispr-yuval-noah-harari-crispr-hmmm-what-would-stalin-have-done-with-that.html

Visit TimeToFreeAmerica.com/TheHomoDeuce to watch the video clips referenced throughout this book.

»**The Klaus Schwab Lead Advisor Praised by Obama, Zuckerberg & Gates, Yuval Noah Harari stated, "When You Realize That the Laws Governing Our Society Are Not Eternal and They Are Just the Imagination of People, This Destabilizes Society."**

WATCH - https://rumble.com/v1w7gsq-yuval-noah-harari-when-you-realize-that-the-laws-governing-our-society-are-.html

»**The Klaus Schwab Lead Advisor Praised by Obama, Zuckerberg & Gates, Yuval Noah Harari stated, "New Religions Will Offer People Happiness, Justice & Eternal Life."**

WATCH - https://rumble.com/vymign-yuval-noah-harari-new-religions-will-offer-people-happiness-justice-and-ete.html

»**The Klaus Schwab Lead Advisor Praised by Obama, Zuckerberg & Gates, Yuval Noah Harari stated, "Algorithms That Can Make Decisions On Your Behalf."**

WATCH - https://rumble.com/v1ob2bf-yuval-noah-harari-algorithms-that-can-make-decisions-on-your-behalf..html

»**The Klaus Schwab Lead Advisor Praised by Obama, Zuckerberg & Gates, Yuval Noah Harari stated, "Free Will Is Incompatible with Scientific Findings."**

– WATCH - https://rumble.com/v1oaxa8-yuval-noah-harari-free-will-is-incompatible-with-scientific-findings..html

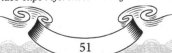

Visit TimeToFreeAmerica.com/TheHomoDeuce to watch the video clips referenced throughout this book.

»The Klaus Schwab Lead Advisor Praised by Obama, Zuckerberg & Gates, Yuval Noah Harari stated, **"The Next Big Project Of Human Kind Will Be to Overcome Old Age & Death... "**

– WATCH - https://rumble.com/v1oamed-yuval-noah-harari-up-grading-humans-into-gods-and-shifting-authority-from-hu.html

»The Klaus Schwab Lead Advisor Praised by Obama, Zuckerberg & Gates, Yuval Noah Harari stated, **"What to Do With Useless People? My Recommendation Is Drugs & Computer Games."**

– WATCH - https://rumble.com/v1oah9d-yuval-noah-harari-what-to-do-with-useless-people-my-recommendation-is-drugs.html

»The Klaus Schwab Lead Advisor Praised by Obama, Zuckerberg & Gates, Yuval Noah Harari stated, **"Brave New World, Which I Think Is The Most Prophetic Book Of The 21st Century."**

– WATCH - https://rumble.com/v1o9hrb-yuval-noah-harari-pope-was-very-helpful-to-push-climate-change-and-jesus-an.html

»The Klaus Schwab Lead Advisor Praised by Obama, Zuckerberg & Gates, Yuval Noah Harari stated, **"My Job Is to Build a Bridge Between the Scientific Community & Public."**

– WATCH - https://rumble.com/v1o9ez8-yuval-noah-harari-my-job-is-to-build-a-bridge-between-the-scientific-commun.html

Visit TimeToFreeAmerica.com/TheHomoDeuce to watch the video clips referenced throughout this book.

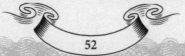

»The Klaus Schwab Lead Advisor Praised by Obama, Zuckerberg & Gates, Yuval Noah Harari stated, **"We Are Entering an Era In Which It Is Possible to Concentrate All of the Information In One Place and Then a Central Command Economy Might Become More Efficient Than a Free Market Capitalist Economy."**

WATCH - https://rumble.com/v108ual-yuval-noah-harari-implementing-a-central-command-economy-and-digitally-base.html

»The Klaus Schwab Lead Advisor Praised by Obama, Zuckerberg & Gates, Yuval Noah Harari stated, **"Human Rights Like God In Heaven, They Are Just a Story Invented by Humans."**

WATCH - https://rumble.com/v106bfy-yuval-noah-harari-klaus-schwab-advisor-explains-why-he-believes-human-right.html

»The Klaus Schwab Lead Advisor Praised by Obama, Zuckerberg & Gates, Yuval Noah Harari stated, **"There Is No Freedom and There Is No Free Will. Google Can Know Me Much Better Than I Know Myself."**

- WATCH - https://rumble.com/v105y8h-yuval-noah-harari-klaus-schwab-advisor-advocates-rejecting-capitalism-voter.html

»The Klaus Schwab Lead Advisor Praised by Obama, Zuckerberg & Gates, Yuval Noah Harari stated, **"Once You Can Hack Humans There Is No Longer Free Will."** '

– *WATCH - https://rumble.com/v103oqi-yuval-noah-harari-klaus-schwab-advisor-once-you-can-hack-humans-there-is-no.html*

»**The Klaus Schwab Lead Advisor Praised by Obama, Zuckerberg & Gates, Yuval Noah Harari stated, "The Next Step, If There Are People Here Who Read Books On Kindle, Then You Probably Know—You SHOULD Know That As You Read The Book, The Book Is Reading YOU. For the First Time In History Books Are Reading People."**

WATCH - "https://rumble.com/v103evl-yuval-noah-harari-klaus-schwab-advisor-introduces-new-religion-data-ism.html

»**The Klaus Schwab Lead Advisor Praised by Obama, Zuckerberg & Gates, Yuval Noah Harari stated, "The Bible Is Fake News," and "As Far As We Know Humans Are For Nothing."**

WATCH - https://rumble.com/v103kxn-yuval-noah-harari-the-bible-is-fake-news-and-why-we-need-a-one-world-global.html

»**The Klaus Schwab Lead Advisor Praised by Obama, Zuckerberg & Gates, Yuval Noah Harari stated, "We Will Use Advanced Technology, Biotechnology, Nano-Technology and Direct Brain Computer Interfaces to Upgrade Homosapiens Into Different Kinds of Beings."**

- WATCH - https://rumble.com/v103cld-yuval-noah-harari-klaus-schwab-advisor-says-we-are-upgrading-homo-sapiens-i.html

Visit TimeToFreeAmerica.com/TheHomoDeuce to watch the video clips referenced throughout this book.

»The Klaus Schwab Lead Advisor Praised by Obama, Zuckerberg & Gates, Yuval Noah Harari stated, "Neither the Gestapo or the KGB Could Do It, Humans Are Now Hackable Animals."

– WATCH - https://rumble.com/vzydg7-yuval-noah-harari-neither-the-gestapo-or-the-kgb-could-do-it-humans-are-now.html

»The Klaus Schwab Lead Advisor Praised by Obama, Zuckerberg & Gates, Yuval Noah Harari stated, "I'm a Historian That Defines History As the Study Not Of the Past, But As the Study of Change Which Covers Also the Present and the Future."

- WATCH - https://rumble.com/vzxl2t-yuval-noah-harari-i-define-history-as-the-study-of-change-the-present-and-t.html

»The Klaus Schwab Lead Advisor Praised by Obama, Zuckerberg & Gates, Yuval Noah Harari stated, "We Might See Another Round of Techno Religions Where Religions Will Promise Eternal Life On Earth with the Help of Technology." And "We Can Develop Anti-Viruses for the Mind."

- WATCH https://rumble.com/v11k34i-yuval-noah-harari-electric-cars-decide-who-dies-and-eternal-life-on-earth-w.html

»Yuval Noah Harari stated, "AI Isn't Hacking Humans Perfectly, But Doesn't Need Perfect."

Visit TimeToFreeAmerica.com/TheHomoDeuce to watch the video clips referenced throughout this book.

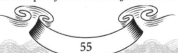

– WATCH - *https://rumble.com/v11jihj-yuval-noah-harari-ai-isnt-hacking-humans-perfectly-but-you-dont-need-perfec.html*

»The Klaus Schwab Lead Advisor Praised by Obama, Zuckerberg & Gates, Yuval Noah Harari stated, "Is It OK to Inflict Pain on COWS In Order to Provide Pleasure for Humans Beings?"

- WATCH - *https://rumble.com/v11dox0-yuval-noah-harari-inside-the-mind-of-the-man-leading-the-great-reset-zucker.html*

»The Klaus Schwab Lead Advisor Praised by Obama, Zuckerberg & Gates, Yuval Noah Harari stated, "Humans Are Hackable Animals... Directly Connecting Brains to Computers."

- WATCH - *https://rumble.com/vxywe3-yuval-noah-harari-humans-are-hackable-animals...directly-connecting-brains-.html*

»The Klaus Schwab Lead Advisor Praised by Obama, Zuckerberg & Gates, Yuval Noah Harari stated, "We Will Have the Ability to Read the Thoughts In the Minds of Another Person Directly Whether They Want It Or Not?"

- WATCH - *https://rumble.com/v1hljt9-yuval-noah-harari-why-did-yuval-noah-harari-say.html*

- KLAUS SCHWAB
"The world will look differently after this transformation."

Visit *TimeToFreeAmerica.com/TheHomoDeuce* to watch
the video clips referenced throughout this book.

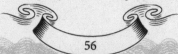

»The Klaus Schwab Lead Advisor Praised by Obama, Zuckerberg & Gates, Yuval Noah Harari stated, "If We Have a New Technology That Makes It Easier for Governments & Corporations to Follow Us and Monitor Us and to Collect Data On Us That Is Fine."

- WATCH - https://rumble.com/v1bwmq5-yuval-noah-harari-.html

»The Klaus Schwab Lead Advisor Praised by Obama, Zuckerberg & Gates, Yuval Noah Harari stated, "When You Talk About Algorithms Taking Over, Algorithms Actually Gather More Power to Themselves. All of the Important Decisions Are Taken By the Algorithm."

- WATCH - https://rumble.com/v1glfdv-yuval-noah-harari-.html

»The Klaus Schwab Lead Advisor Praised by Obama, Zuckerberg & Gates, Yuval Noah Harari stated, "Hitler and the Nazis Knew They Needed Millions of Poor Germans. But, May Be Entering Into an Era Where the Masses Are Not Useful for Anything."

- WATCH - https://rumble.com/v1b32pp-yuval-noah-harari-hitler-and-the-nazis-knew-they-needed-millions-of-poor-ge.html

»The Klaus Schwab Lead Advisor Praised by Obama, Zuckerberg & Gates, Yuval Noah Harari stated, "We Now Have the Technology to Hack the Human Brain. Hitler Couldn't Know Everyone's Reaction, Now It's Feasible. Not Just Feasible, It's Happening."

Visit TimeToFreeAmerica.com/TheHomoDeuce to watch the video clips referenced throughout this book.

- *WATCH - https://rumble.com/v1358z3-yuval-noah-harari-hit-ler-couldnt-know-everyones-reaction-now-its-feasible..html*

»**The Klaus Schwab Lead Advisor Praised by Obama, Zuckerberg & Gates, Yuval Noah Harari stated, "The Nature of Money Is Going to Change Dramatically. The Old Systems of Ownership and Trust Will Have to Adapt Radically."**

- *WATCH - https://rumble.com/v1c8yhz-yuval-no-ah-harari-interview-with-christine-legarde.html*

»**The Klaus Schwab Lead Advisor Praised by Obama, Zuckerberg & Gates, Yuval Noah Harari stated, "We Don't Have to Wait Until Christ's Second Coming to Overcome Death. A Couple of Geeks Can Do It If You Give Them Enough Time and Money. God Is Dead, It Just Takes Awhile to Get Rid of the Body. I Don't Think Life Has Any Meaning."**

- *WATCH - https://rumble.com/v1coonb-yuval-noah-harari-god-is-dead-it-just-takes-awhile-to-get-rid-of-the-body-m.html*

»**The Klaus Schwab Lead Advisor Praised by Obama, Zuckerberg & Gates, Yuval Noah Harari stated, "We Are Facing These Major Problems That Just Cannot Be Solved without Global Cooperation."**

- *WATCH - https://rumble.com/v1muvkk-yuval-noah-harari-.html*

Visit TimeToFreeAmerica.com/TheHomoDeuce to watch the video clips referenced throughout this book.

»**The Klaus Schwab Lead Advisor Praised by Obama, Zuckerberg & Gates, Yuval Noah Harari stated, "Liberal Democracy Has Been Based Upon a Misunderstanding of Human Nature. It Was OK to Believe In This Myth, But Now It's Falling Apart."**

- WATCH - https://rumble.com/v1b2nir-yuval-noah-harari-liberal-democracy-has-been-based-upon-a-misunderstanding-.html

»**The Klaus Schwab Lead Advisor Praised by Obama, Zuckerberg & Gates, Yuval Noah Harari stated, "The Issue of Whether the Climate Crisis Is Real That's a Purely Scientific Issue. It's Not a Matter for Politicians or Even for Voters to Say If It's Real or Not."**

- WATCH - https://rumble.com/v1cmdsj-yuval-noah-harari-.html

»**The Klaus Schwab Lead Advisor Praised by Obama, Zuckerberg & Gates, Yuval Noah Harari stated, "Authority Will Shift from Individuals to the Wisdom of External Algorithms." and "In Silicon Valley Equality Is Out, But Immorality Is In"**

– WATCH - https://rumble.com/v11cvny-yuval-noah-harari-equality-is-out-but-immortality-is-in..html

»**The Klaus Schwab Lead Advisor Praised by Obama, Zuckerberg & Gates, Yuval Noah Harari stated, "Biotechnology & Artificial Intelligence Will Change What It Means to Be Human."**

Visit TimeToFreeAmerica.com/TheHomoDeuce to watch the video clips referenced throughout this book.

– WATCH - *https://rumble.com/v11cnsz-yuval-noah-harari-bio-technology-and-artificial-intelligence-will-change-wha.html*

....

»**The Klaus Schwab Lead Advisor Praised by Obama, Zuckerberg & Gates, Yuval Noah Harari stated, "In All Likelihood Our (Human) Species Is Going to Disappear?"**

- WATCH - *https://rumble.com/v1ev39h-yu-val-noah-harari-why-did-yuval-say.html*

....

»**The Klaus Schwab Lead Advisor Praised by Obama, Zuckerberg & Gates, Yuval Noah Harari stated, "There Is No Reason Why Christianity Became the Dominant Religion"**

– WATCH - *https://rumble.com/v11ckmq-yuval-noah-hara-ri-there-is-no-reason-why-christianity-became-the-dominant-r.html*

....

»**The Klaus Schwab Lead Advisor Praised by Obama, Zuckerberg & Gates, Yuval Noah Harari stated, "We Are Now Basically the Gods of Planet Earth."**

– WATCH - *https://rumble.com/v11bb6c-yuval-noah-harari-wef-lead-advisor-we-are-now-basically-the-gods-of-planet-.html*

....

»**The Klaus Schwab Lead Advisor Praised by Obama, Zuckerberg & Gates, Yuval Noah Harari stated, "Silicon Valley, This Is Where the New Religions Are Being Created by People Like Ray Kurzweil. These Are the Religions That Will Take Over the World."**

- WATCH - *https://rumble.com/v1chaj1-yuval-noah-harari-.html*

....

*Visit TimeToFreeAmerica.com/TheHomoDeuce to watch
the video clips referenced throughout this book.*

»The Klaus Schwab Lead Advisor Praised by Obama, Zuckerberg & Gates, Yuval Noah Harari stated, "There Is No Point Teaching People In School Specific Information. They Can Google It."

- WATCH - https://rumble.com/v1muv6y-yuval-noah-harari-.html

»The Klaus Schwab Lead Advisor Praised by Obama, Zuckerberg & Gates, Yuval Noah Harari stated, "There Is No Reason Why Genetic Engineering Couldn't Create Super Human and Genius Humans. The Main Obstacles On the Way to Creating Superhumans Are Ethical and Political. It Is Very Hard to See How They Could Hold Back the Next Step In the Process Indefinitely. What Is At Stake Here Is Prolonging Human Life Indefinitely."

- WATCH - https://rumble.com/v1evgr1-yuval-noah-harari-2013.html

»The Klaus Schwab Lead Advisor Praised by Obama, Zuckerberg & Gates, Yuval Noah Harari stated, "We Are One of the Last Chapters in the Story of Homo Sapiens."

– WATCH - https://rumble.com/v1144c0-yuval-noah-harari-we-are-one-of-the-last-chapters-in-the-story-of-homo-sapi.html

YUVAL NOAH HARARI
"Nationalism Is a Barrier for Cooperation On the International Level. The President of the U.S. (Trump) Said That There Is a Contradiction Between Nationalism and Globalism and That People Should Choose Nationalism."

Visit TimeToFreeAmerica.com/TheHomoDeuce to watch the video clips referenced throughout this book.

»The Klaus Schwab Lead Advisor Praised by Obama, Zuckerberg & Gates, Yuval Noah Harari stated, **"God Is Dead It Just Takes Awhile to Get Rid of the Body." Says WEF Advisor.**

– WATCH - https://rumble.com/v10d4oo-yuval-noah-harari-god-is-dead-it-just-takes-awhile-to-get-rid-of-the-body.-.html

»The Klaus Schwab Lead Advisor Praised by Obama, Zuckerberg & Gates, Yuval Noah Harari stated, **"What Does It Mean to Live Life Where Decisions Are Managed by Outside Systems?"**

– WATCH - https://rumble.com/v1141t9-yuval-noah-harari-what-does-it-mean-to-live-life-where-decisions-are-manage.html

»The Klaus Schwab Lead Advisor Praised by Obama, Zuckerberg & Gates, Yuval Noah Harari stated, **"Once You Can Hack Human Beings, Then Authority Is Likely To Shift From Human Feelings To Algorithms. And Humanisms, And Elections, And The Free Market And So On—All This Will Make No More Sense."**

– WATCH - https://rumble.com/v10do4h-yuval-noah-harari-the-easiest-people-to-manipulate-are-people-that-believe-.html

»The Klaus Schwab Lead Advisor Praised by Obama, Zuckerberg & Gates, Yuval Noah Harari stated, **"Free Will Is Incompatible with Scientific Findings."**

- WATCH - https://rumble.com/v10axa8-yuval-noah-harari-free-will-is-incompatible-with-scientific-findings..html

Visit TimeToFreeAmerica.com/TheHomoDeuce to watch the video clips referenced throughout this book.

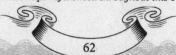

»**The Klaus Schwab Lead Advisor Praised by Obama, Zuckerberg & Gates, Yuval Noah Harari stated, "Biological Knowledge Multiplied By Computing Power Multiplied By Data Equals the Ability To Hack Humans."**

- WATCH - https://rumble.com/vy18k5-yuval-noah-harari-hacking-humans-and-shifting-authority-from-humans-to-algo.html

»**The Klaus Schwab Lead Advisor Praised by Obama, Zuckerberg & Gates, Yuval Noah Harari stated, "In Places Like Silicon Valley Equality Is Out, But Immortality Is In. We Don't Have to Wait for the Second Coming of Christ to Overcome Death."**

- WATCH - https://rumble.com/v1igrqj-yuval-noah-harari-.html

» **Yuval Noah Harari stated, "The Same Surveillance That Can Tell Whether You Have Covid-19 Can Also Tell When You're Angry, When You're Joyful, When You're Bored."**

- WATCH - https://rumble.com/vy525f-yuval-noah-harari-surveillance-under-the-skin-and-trusting-science-above-ev.html

»**The Klaus Schwab Lead Advisor Praised by Obama, Zuckerberg & Gates, Yuval Noah Harari stated, "Corporations and Governments Are Collecting Data About Where We Go, Who We Meet and What Movies We Watch. The Next Phase In Surveillance Under the Skin."**

– WATCH - https://rumble.com/vxhikf-yuval-noah-harari-the-next-stage-is-surveillance-under-the-skin.-says-lead-.html

Visit TimeToFreeAmerica.com/TheHomoDeuce to watch the video clips referenced throughout this book.

»The Klaus Schwab Lead Advisor Praised by Obama, Zuckerberg & Gates, Yuval Noah Harari stated, **"New Surveillance Technologies That Are Now Deployed Just To Deal With This Coronavirus Outbreak—When It's Over, Some Governments May Say... Why Not Protect People Against [Other Threats] With This New Surveillance System. So The Tendency Would Be To Prolong It Indefinitely."**

- Watch – https://rumble.com/vxgprz-yuval-noah-harari-sensors-in-bodies-will-allow-google-facebook-chinese-gov-.html

»The Klaus Schwab Lead Advisor Praised by Obama, Zuckerberg & Gates, Yuval Noah Harari stated, **"The Whole Idea That Humans Have This Spirit or Soul Or That They Have Free Will and Nobody Knows What Is Happening Inside Me or Whatever I Choose Whether In the Election or Whether In the Supermarket This Is My Free Will, That's Over."**

- WATCH - https://rumble.com/vxgprz-yuval-noah-harari-sensors-in-bodies-will-allow-google-facebook-chinese-gov-.html

»The Klaus Schwab Lead Advisor Praised by Obama, Zuckerberg & Gates, Yuval Noah Harari stated, **"We Have the Technology to Hack Human Beings On a Massive Scale."**

– WATCH - https://rumble.com/vxhikf-yuval-noah-harari-the-next-stage-is-surveillance-under-the-skin.-says-lead-.html

Visit TimeToFreeAmerica.com/TheHomoDeuce to watch the video clips referenced throughout this book.

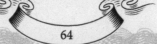

»The Klaus Schwab Lead Advisor Praised by Obama, Zuckerberg & Gates, Yuval Noah Harari stated, **"We Need Some Kind of Global Loyalty and Global Identity."**

- WATCH - https://rumble.com/vxe57j-yuval-noah-harari-we-are-in-the-process-of-becoming-gods-and-we-need-some-t.html

»The Klaus Schwab Lead Advisor Praised by Obama, Zuckerberg & Gates, Yuval Noah Harari stated, **"There Is No Such Thing As Free Will. Humans Have Invented God."**

- WATCH - https://rumble.com/vxcgaf-yuval-noah-harari-there-is-no-such-thing-as-free-will-and-humans-have-inven.html

»The Klaus Schwab Lead Advisor Praised by Obama, Zuckerberg & Gates, Yuval Noah Harari stated, **"Free Will Is Over."**

– WATCH – https://rumble.com/vthdl6-the-evil-transhumanism-agenda-of-klaus-schwab-and-doctor-yuval-noah-harari.html

»The Klaus Schwab Lead Advisor Praised by Obama, Zuckerberg & Gates, Yuval Noah Harari stated, **"Free Will Is a Theological Mistake."**

WATCH – https://rumble.com/vy5ejj-yuval-noah-harari-free-will-is-a-theological-mistake-and-hacking-humans.html

Visit TimeToFreeAmerica.com/TheHomoDeuce to watch the video clips referenced throughout this book.

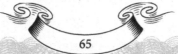

»The Klaus Schwab Lead Advisor Praised by Obama, Zuckerberg & Gates, Yuval Noah Harari stated, **"Freedom Has Absolutely No Meaning from a Physical or Biological Perspective. It Is Just Another Myth, Another Term That Humans Have Invented. Humans Have Invented God and Humans Have Invented Heaven and Hell and Humans Have Invented Free-Will."**

- WATCH - https://rumble.com/vxcgaf-yuval-noah-harari-there-is-no-such-thing-as-free-will-and-humans-have-inven.html

»The Klaus Schwab Lead Advisor Praised by Obama, Zuckerberg & Gates, Yuval Noah Harari stated, **"And Now If You Give the Tools to Start Changing or Ovecoming Biology, Just Think About Sex Life. Almost Every Religion and Every Ideology Wanted to Limit Human Sexuality. Now Think If You Can Really Start Messing with Human Biology, What Will Be the Result of These Sexual Fantasies?" – Yuval Noah Harari**

- Watch – https://rumble.com/vxee5z-yuval-noah-harari-if-you-have-the-tools-to-overcome-human-biology...think-a.html

»Yuval Noah Harari Stated: **"Now The Main Thing We Want To Know Is In The Body. We Want To Know If You're Sick Or Not. Whether You Have COVID-19. What's Your Body Temperature? Your Blood Pressure, Your Heart Rate. And This Changes the Nature Of Surveillance."**

- WATCH – https://rumble.com/vy525f-yuval-noah-harari-surveillance-under-the-skin-and-trusting-science-abo

*Visit TimeToFreeAmerica.com/TheHomoDeuce to watch
the video clips referenced throughout this book.*

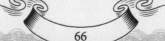

»**The Klaus Schwab Lead Advisor Praised by Obama, Zuckerberg & Gates, Yuval Noah Harari stated, "Everybody In the Country 24 Hours Per Day Are Being Surveyed by These Very Powerful Technologies and This Results In Decisions About Everything."**

– WATCH – https://rumble.com/vy4xyl-yuval-noah-harari-klaus-schwab-advisor-advocating-genetically-modified-babi.html

»**The Klaus Schwab Lead Advisor Praised by Obama, Zuckerberg & Gates, Yuval Noah Harari stated, "Long-Term We Should Try to Reimagine a Different System and a Different Set of Values. Hacking Humans and Shifting Authority from Humans to Algorithms."**

– WATCH – https://rumble.com/vy18k5-yuval-noah-harari-hacking-humans-and-shifting-authority-from-humans-to-algo.html

»**The Klaus Schwab Lead Advisor Praised by Obama, Zuckerberg & Gates, Yuval Noah Harari stated, "We Need to Work with the BEAST and Not Against It."**

– WATCH – https://rumble.com/vy129f-yuval-noah-harari-we-need-to-work-with-the-beast-and-not-against-it.html

»**The Klaus Schwab Lead Advisor Praised by Obama, Zuckerberg & Gates, Yuval Noah Harari stated, "If We Shift the Authority to Make Decisions to the A.I., the A.I. Votes, the A.I. Chooses."**

Visit TimeToFreeAmerica.com/TheHomoDeuce to watch the video clips referenced throughout this book.

- WATCH - https://rumble.com/vyonep-yuval-noah-harari-yuval-advocates-allowing-artificial-intelligence-to-vote-.html

»**The Klaus Schwab Lead Advisor Praised by Obama, Zuckerberg & Gates, Yuval Noah Harari stated, "We Are Upgrading Humans Into Gods"**

– WATCH – https://rumble.com/vy126n-yuval-noah-harari-we-are-upgrading-humans-into-gods.html

»**Yuval Noah Harari stated, "We Are On the Verge of Creating the First Inorganic Life Forms"**

– WATCH – https://rumble.com/vyovtt-yuval-noah-harari-we-are-on-the-verge-of-creating-the-first-inorganic-life-.html

»**Yuval Noah Harari stated, "They Can Develop an Anti-Virus for the Mind. We Need to Develop an Anti-Virus for the Mind."**

– WATCH – https://rumble.com/vyooj9-yuval-noah-harari-creating-an-anti-virus-for-the-mind-and-the-basic-premise.html

»**Yuval Noah Harari w/ Huawei CEO Banned by Trump, "The Really Big Thing Is Hacking Human Beings."**

– WATCH – https://rumble.com/vyomkh-yuval-noah-harari-w-huawei-ceo-banned-by-trump-hacking-humans-inheriting-so.html

Visit TimeToFreeAmerica.com/TheHomoDeuce to watch the video clips referenced throughout this book.

»The Klaus Schwab Lead Advisor Praised by Obama, Zuckerberg & Gates, Yuval Noah Harari stated, "Surveillance Is Going Under the Skin. We See a Change In the Nature of Surveillance. Previously Surveillance Was Above the Skin, Now It's Going Under the Skin."

- WATCH - https://rumble.com/vy0l1z-yuval-noah-harari-surveillance-is-going-under-the-skin..html

»The Klaus Schwab Lead Advisor Praised by Obama, Zuckerberg & Gates, Yuval Noah Harari stated, "Jesus Rising from the Dead and Being the Son of God, This Is FAKE NEWS."

– WATCH – https://rumble.com/vxz099-yuval-noah-harari-yuval-states-jesus-rising-from-the-dead-and-being-the-son.html

»The Klaus Schwab Lead Advisor Praised by Obama, Zuckerberg & Gates, Yuval Noah Harari stated, "Humans Are Now Hackable Animals. Whatever Replaces Us It Will Be Different from Us, Much More Than We Are Different from Neanderthals. "

– WATCH – https://rumble.com/vxywe3-yuval-noah-harari-humans-are-hackable-animals...directly-connecting-brains-.html

YUVAL NOAH HARARI

"Trump Is Destroying the U.S. Alliance System All Over the World. He's Destroying the Greatest Achievement of the U.S. Foreign Policy for Decades to Build This Global Alliance System."

Visit TimeToFreeAmerica.com/TheHomoDeuce to watch the video clips referenced throughout this book.

»The Klaus Schwab Lead Advisor Praised by Obama, Zuckerberg & Gates, Yuval Noah Harari stated, **"In the Coming Years We Will Face Individual Discrimination...And You Will Not Be Able to Do Anything Against This Discrimination."**

– WATCH – *https://rumble.com/vxyslr-yuval-noah-harari-in-the-future-you-will-face-discrimination-based-on-a-goo.html*

»The Klaus Schwab Lead Advisor Praised by Obama, Zuckerberg & Gates, Yuval Noah Harari stated, **"Most Legal Systems Today Are Based On a Belief in Human Rights. Human Rights Just Like God In Heaven Are a Story That We've Invented."**

https://rumble.com/vxyrp7-yuval-noah-harari-yuval-argues-against-gods-existence-human-rights-national.html

WHY DO "ELITES" OFTEN REFER TO YUVAH NOAH HARARI AS A PROPHET?

WATCH – *https://rumble.com/vxynrv-yuval-noah-harari-why-do-elites-often-refer-to-yuvah-noah-harari-as-a-proph.html*

»The Klaus Schwab Lead Advisor Praised by Obama, Zuckerberg & Gates, Yuval Noah Harari stated, **"Economies in the Future Where Humans Are Not Needed Even As Consumers."**

– WATCH – *https://rumble.com/vxyl7n-yuval-noval-harari-economies-in-the-future-where-humans-are-not-needed-even.html*

Visit TimeToFreeAmerica.com/TheHomoDeuce to watch the video clips referenced throughout this book.

»The Klaus Schwab Lead Advisor Praised by Obama, Zuckerberg & Gates, Yuval Noah Harari stated, **"Having The Ability To Monitor People Under The Skin—This Is the Biggest Game-Changer Of All."**

– WATCH – https://rumble.com/vxyfo5-yuval-noah-harari-the-covid-crisis-was-the-moment-when-surveillance-started.html

»The Klaus Schwab Lead Advisor Praised by Obama, Zuckerberg & Gates, Yuval Noah Harari stated, **"Dictators Always Dreamt About It... It's NOW Possible to Eliminate Privacy."**

– WATCH – https://rumble.com/vxyf7r-yuval-noah-harari-dictators-always-dreamt-about-it...its-now-possible-to-el.html

»The Klaus Schwab Lead Advisor Praised by Obama, Zuckerberg & Gates, Yuval Noah Harari stated, **"The Ultimate Value of Humans Will Be Just As Consumers That Will Do Nothing Useful At All."**

– WATCH – https://rumble.com/vxxnex-yuval-noah-harari-they-trade-and-make-billions-of-dollars-and-you-dont-use-.html

»The Klaus Schwab Lead Advisor Praised by Obama, Zuckerberg & Gates, Yuval Noah Harari stated, **"The Bank Rejected You for a Loan and You Will Not Be Able to Understand. An Algorithm Is Able to Take In Thousands and Thousands of Data Points. The Algorithm Went Over All of This and Calculated Why You Are Not Credit Worthy."**

Visit TimeToFreeAmerica.com/TheHomoDeuce to watch the video clips referenced throughout this book.

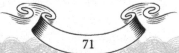

- WATCH - https://rumble.com/vxeccf-yuval-noah-harari-ex-plains-the-social-credit-score-system-which-is-coming-s.html

»**The Klaus Schwab Lead Advisor Praised by Obama, Zuckerberg & Gates, Yuval Noah Harari stated, "You Cannot Break the Rules of Nature. If Homosexuality Was Against Nature It Just Couldn't Exist."**

- WATCH – https://rumble.com/vxebkn-yuvah-noah-harari-you-cannot-violate-the-rules-of-nature-lead-advisor-for-k.html

»**The Klaus Schwab Lead Advisor Praised by Obama, Zuckerberg & Gates, Yuval Noah Harari stated, "If You Thought That the Bible Was the Highest Source of Authority, Then the Main Purpose of Education Was to Teach You What God Said and What the Bible Said. In Humanist Education, Since the Highest Source Authority Is Your Own Feelings and Your Own Thoughts, the Chief Aim of Education Is to Enable You to Think for Yourself."**

- WATCH - https://rumble.com/vxcffn-yuval-noah-harari-feel-ings-are-the-ultimate-source-of-authority-lead-adviso.html

»**Yuval Noah Harari stated, "What Is Good and What Is Evil? In Previous Eras You Went to God or You Went to the Bible. And This Was the Source of Ethical Authority. Now In the Era of Humanist Ethics, the Saying Is We Don't Care Very Much What God Says We Want to Know What People Feel. The Highest Authority In the Field of Human Ethics Is Human Feelings."**

Visit TimeToFreeAmerica.com/TheHomoDeuce to watch the video clips referenced throughout this book.

- WATCH - https://rumble.com/vxcet5-yuval-noah-harari-lead-advisor-for-klaus-schwab-argues-against-the-bible-an.html

»**The Klaus Schwab Lead Advisor Praised by Obama, Zuckerberg & Gates, Yuval Noah Harari stated, "We Need an Antivirus for the Brain."**

– WATCH – https://rumble.com/vxcdkz-yuval-noah-harari-top-advisor-for-klaus-schwab-explains-we-need-a-anti-viru.html

»**The Klaus Schwab Lead Advisor Praised by Obama, Zuckerberg & Gates, Yuval Noah Harari stated to Mark Zuckerberg "Is It Still True That the Voter Knows Best or Have We Gone Past This Point?"**

– WATCH – https://rumble.com/vxcc01-yuval-noah-harari-interview-w-mark-zuckerberg-is-still-true-that-the-voter-.html

»**The Klaus Schwab Lead Advisor Praised by Obama, Zuckerberg & Gates, Yuval Noah Harari stated, "Now In the Past Many Tyrants Wanted to Do It, But Nobody Understood Biology Well Enough and Nobody Had Enough Computing Power and Data to Hack Millions of People. Neither the Gestapo nor the KBG Could Do It, But Soon At Least Some Corporations and Governments Will Be Able to Systematically Hack All of the People."**

WATCH - https://rumble.com/vwtgvx-yuval-noah-harari-how-can-we-get-global-agreement-on-ai-w-putin-in-ukraine.html

Visit TimeToFreeAmerica.com/TheHomoDeuce to watch the video clips referenced throughout this book.

»Klaus Schwab Lead Advisor Praised by Obama, Zuckerberg & Gates, Yuval Noah Harari stated, "The Entire Legal Democratic System Is Built On Philosophical Ideas We've Inherited From the 18th Century—Especially the Idea of Free Will..."

- WATCH - https://rumble.com/v1xaeei-yuval-noah-harari-free-will-has-always-been-a-myth..html

»Klaus Schwab Lead Advisor Praised by Obama, Zuckerberg & Gates, Yuval Noah Harari stated, "We Will Learn How to Engineer Bodies, Brains and Minds. These Will Be the Main Products of the 21st Century Economy. How Will the Future Masters of the Planet Look Like? This Will Be Decided By the People Who Own the Data."

- WATCH - https://rumble.com/v1x9era-yuval-noah-harari-we-will-learn-how-to-engineer-bodies.html

» Klaus Schwab Lead Advisor Praised by Obama, Zuckerberg & Gates, Yuval Noah Harari stated, "Now We Are Gaining This Power to Create Life Just Like God, and In a Way We Even Go Beyond the Biblical God. The Only Thing God Managed to Create Are Organic Beings."

- WATCH - https://rumble.com/v1x91ic-yuval-noah-harari-now-we-are-gaining-this-power-to-create-life-just-like-go.html

Visit TimeToFreeAmerica.com/TheHomoDeuce to watch the video clips referenced throughout this book.

» **Klaus Schwab Lead Advisor Praised by Obama, Zuckerberg & Gates, Yuval Noah Harari stated, "Should Robots Have Rights? Should A.I. Be Authorized to Make Ethical Decisions? Should We Produce Autonomous Weapon Systems That Can Decide On Their Own Initiative Who to Kill?"**

- WATCH - https://rumble.com/v1x50lu-yuval-noah-harari-should-robots-have-rights.html

» **Klaus Schwab Lead Advisor Praised by Obama, Zuckerberg & Gates, Yuval Noah Harari stated, "Think of the Potential Impact of Having a Scale of Consciousness Within Humanity Itself Which Places Some Humans or Some Feelings Above Other Humans and Others Feelings. What Will That Do to Voting Rights?"**

- WATCH - https://rumble.com/v1x5020-yuval-noah-harari-elections-and-voting-rights-think-of-the-potential.html

» **Klaus Schwab Lead Advisor Praised by Obama, Zuckerberg & Gates, Yuval Noah Harari stated, "Most People Believe That Humans Have Some Kind of Superior Consciousness Which Justifies the Way We Treat Billions of Other Animals. This Unproven Theory May Have Caused More Suffering Than Any Other Single Idea In the Whole of History."**

- WATCH - https://rumble.com/v1x4zg6-yuval-noah-harari-meat-consumption-most-people-believe-that-humans.html

Visit TimeToFreeAmerica.com/TheHomoDeuce to watch the video clips referenced throughout this book.

»Klaus Schwab Lead Advisor Praised by Obama, Zuckerberg & Gates, Yuval Noah Harari stated, "If Two Men Love Each Other How Does This Harm Anyone? Ethics and Politics Are No Longer About Divine Commandments Or Alleged Laws of Nature, They Are About Feelings."

- WATCH - https://rumble.com/v1x4xko-yuval-noah-harari-if-two-men-love-each-other-how-does-this-harm.html

»Klaus Schwab Lead Advisor Praised by Obama, Zuckerberg & Gates, Yuval Noah Harari stated, "Humanity Has the Power to Prevent Catastrophic Climate Change. If We Invest 2% of Global GDP, We Can Prevent Catastrophic Climate Change."

- WATCH - https://rumble.com/v1x4ino-yuval-noah-harari-humanity-has-the-power-to-prevent-catastrophic.html

PROGRAMMABLE CENTRAL BANK DIGITAL CURRENCIES ARE HERE NOW!

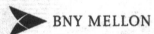

Banking Giants & New York Fed Start 12-Week Digital Dollar Pilot.

Visit TimeToFreeAmerica.com/TheHomoDeuce to watch the video clips referenced throughout this book.

"The Fourth Industrial Revolution changes you, if you take a genetic editing..."

- KLAUS SCHWAB

Visit *TimeToFreeAmerica.com/TheHomoDeuce to watch the video clips referenced throughout this book.*

CHAPTER 4:

What Has Klaus Schwab Actually Stated About the Future?

WHAT IS THE HISTORY OF THE WORLD ECONOMIC FORUM?

World Economic Forum headquarters in Geneva, Switzerland

Started in 1971 and based in Geneva, Switzerland. It consists of 600 + highly educated people around the world. Members include World leaders, religious leaders, scientists, media, etc.

Visit TimeToFreeAmerica.com/TheHomoDeuce to watch the video clips referenced throughout this book.

Davos is the informal name of the annual four-day conference held by The World Economic Forum. Celebrities that attend include: Bono, Leonardo DiCaprio, Justin Trudeau, Joe Biden, Mark Zuckerberg, Bill Gates, Sergey Brin, Charlize Theron, Bill Clinton, Angelina Jolie, Prince William, Cate Blanchett, Chinese President Xi Jinping, Matt Damon, King Charles, John Kerry, Shakira, Arianna Huffington, and more.

WHO IS KLAUS SCHWAB?

Klaus Schwab's father was a Nazi who served the Third Reich war effort as the director of Escher Wyss AG, an industrial company that manufactured flamethrowers to kill Allied soldiers. Professor Klaus Schwab was born in Ravensburg, Germany in 1938. He is Founder and Executive Chairman of the World Economic Forum, the International Organization for Public-Private Cooperation which he started per the recommendation of Henry Kissinger In 1971.

Schwab attended 1st and 2nd grade at the primary school in the Wädenswil district of Au ZH, in Switzerland. After World War Two, his family moved back to Germany where Schwab attended the Spohn-Gymnasium in Ravensburg until his Abitur in 1957

In 1961, he graduated as a mechanical engineer from Swiss Federal Institute of Technology in Zurich, which awarded him a doctorate in engineering. He was also awarded a doctorate in economics from the University of Fribourg, and a Master of Public Administration degree from the John F. Kennedy School of Government at Harvard University.

Klaus Schwab's mentors were the leaders in America's thermo nuclear deterrence program. (See Reece report)

Henry Kissenger, John K. Galbraith (an economist at Harvard who studied Hitler's National Socialist government policies), and Herman Kahn, who wanted to subvert democracy by training a group of world government young leaders.

READ MORE – https://washingtontimes.com/news/2022/ may/25/in-davos-global-elites-conspire-to-take-away-your-/

WHAT HAS KLAUS SCHWAB ACTUALLY SAID ABOUT THE FUTURE?

»**Klaus Schwab stated, "When You See the Book of Professor Harari Homo Deus..The New Technologies Will Change (Humans) Us. It Is the Fusion of the Physical, Biological and Digital Worlds."**

Visit TimeToFreeAmerica.com/TheHomoDeuce to watch the video clips referenced throughout this book.

- WATCH - https://rumble.com/v1gxygf-the-great-reset-klaus-schwab-says-.html

»**Klaus Schwab stated, "Certainly In the Next 10 Years We Could Imagine That We Will Implant Them In Our Brains and In Our Skin and In the End Maybe There Will Be a Direct Communication Between Our Brain and the Digital World."**

- WATCH - https://rumble.com/vvqqpn-the-great-reset-vs-the-great-reawakening-the-transhumanism-nano-tech-agenda.html

»**Klaus Schwab has stated, "You will own nothing and be happy.**

»**Klaus Schwab has stated, "The Fourth Industrial Revolution Changes You If You Take the Gene-Editing."**

- WATCH - https://rumble.com/v1s26du-yuval-noah-hara-ri-klaus-schwab-lead-advisor-and-klaus-schwab.html

»**Klaus Schwab has stated, "Joe Biden Is One of the Most Engaged and Hardest Working Members Here At the Annual (World Economic Forum) Meeting."**

- WATCH - https://rumble.com/v1itvsx-joe-biden-why-did-biden.html

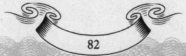

»Klaus Schwab has stated, "We have continuous partnerships with many governments around the world... Then of course, we have NGOs, we have trade unions, we have all those different parts – media, of course – and very important experts and scientists and academia...religious leaders, social entrepreneurs..."

- WATCH - https://rumble.com/vu4wjm-klaus-schwab-says-he-controls-religious-leaders-media-scientists-experts-et.html

https://rumble.com/v1x5hb2-klaus-schwab-the-world-economic-forum-is-now-600-highly-educated-people-loc.html

Yuval - TRUMP Klaus - TRUMP

»Klaus Schwab Has Stated, "And I Have to Say When I Mention Now Names Like Mrs. Merkel, even Vladimir Putin, and So On They Have All Been Members of the Young Global Leaders of the World Economic Forum. But We Are Very Proud of the Young Generation, Like Prime Minister Trudeau, the President of Argentina and So On. We Have Penetrated the Cabinets. I Know That Half of Trudeau's Cabinet Are Young Global Leaders of the World Economic Forum."

– WATCH - https://rumble.com/vvqqpn-the-great-reset-vs-the-great-reawakening-the-transhumanism-nano-tech-agenda.html

KLAUS SCHWAB

"We Do Know That Global Energy Systems, Food Systems and Supply Chains Will Be Deeply Affected." That People Should Choose Nationalism."

Visit TimeToFreeAmerica.com/TheHomoDeuce to watch the video clips referenced throughout this book.

»**Klaus Schwab stated, "It Is a Job Destroyer. The Fourth Industrial Revolution Is Like a Tsunami."**

- WATCH - https://rumble.com/v1nxm9g-klaus-schwab-it-is-a-job-destroyer.-the-fourth-industrial-revolution-is-lik.html

»**Klaus Schwab stated, The Great Reset "We Are In the Midst of the Fourth Industrial Revolution."**

- WATCH - https://rumble.com/v1lpeqn-klaus-schwab-the-great-reset-we-are-in-the-midst-of-the-fourth-industrial-r.html

»**Klaus Schwab stated, "We Will Not Go Back to Normal."**

- WATCH - https://rumble.com/vu66h8-the-great-reset-author-klaus-schwab-states-we-will-not-go-back-to-normal..html

»**Klaus Schwab stated, "We Have to Take More Advantage of the Technologies of the Fourth Industrial Revolution- Artificial Intelligence, Genetic-Engineering, etc."**

- WATCH - https://rumble.com/v1jeun9-klaus-schwab-we-have-to-take-more.html

»**Klaus Schwab stated, "We Are Moving the World from a Unipolar to a Multipolar World and China Plays an Enormous Role?"**

- WATCH - https://rumble.com/v1h67qp-klaus-schwab-why-did-klaus-schwab-say-we-are-moving-the-world-from-a-unipol.html

Visit TimeToFreeAmerica.com/TheHomoDeuce to watch the video clips referenced throughout this book.

»**Klaus Schwab stated, "We Must Be Prepared for an Angrier World."**

   - *WATCH - https://rumble.com/v1aboat-klaus-schwab-we-must-prepare-for-an-angrier-world.html*

»**Klaus Schwab stated, "The Great Reset 4th Industrial Revolution Has Become a Reality."**

   - *WATCH - https://rumble.com/v11d2g7-klaus-schwab-the-great-reset-4th-industrial-revolution-has-become-a-reality.html*

»**Klaus Schwab stated, "Nobody Will Be Safe If Not Everybody Is Vaccinated."**

   - *WATCH - https://rumble.com/v10mf5h-klaus-schwab-nobody-will-be-safe-if-not-everybody-is-vaccinated-global-weal.html*

»**Klaus Schwab stated, Klaus Schwab & Yuval Noah Harari | "I Am Convinced That We Will Destroy A lot of Employment, Just Look At the Bank Employees and So On…If You Are Left Behind They Won't Even Need You As a Serf or a Slave."**

   - *WATCH - https://rumble.com/v1k1vep-klaus-schwab-and-yuval-noah-harari-i-am-convinced-that-we-will.html*

»**Klaus Schwab stated, "The Fourth Industrial Revolution Changes Who We Are."**

- WATCH - https://rumble.com/v18xb2f-klaus-schwab-the-fourth-industrial-revolution-changes-who-we-are.html

»**Klaus Schwab stated, "The Fourth Industrial Revolution Will Lead to the Fusion of Our Physical, Digital and Biological Identities."**

- WATCH - https://rumble.com/vuc101-klaus-schwab-the-great-reset-is-the-fusion-of-our-physical-digital-and-biol.html

»**Klaus Schwab stated, "The Fourth Industrial Revolution Will Impact Our Lives Completely. It Will Actually Change Us, Our Own Identities."**

- WATCH - https://rumble.com/vu656a-klaus-schwab-the-great-reset-will-change-actually-own-and-our-own-identity.html

»**Klaus Schwab stated, "The World Economic Forum Consists of 600 Highly-Educated People Located Around the World."**

WATCH - https://rumble.com/v11sw6r-klaus-schwab-explains-the-great-reset-agenda-600-highly-educated-people-loc.html

Visit TimeToFreeAmerica.com/TheHomoDeuce to watch the video clips referenced throughout this book.

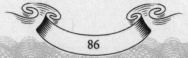

»Klaus Schwab stated, "What We Have to Confront Is a Deep Systemic and Structural Restructuring of Our World and This Will Take Some Time and the World Will Look Differently After We Have Gone Through This Transformation Process. A Transition Into a Multi-Polar World."

- WATCH - https://rumble.com/v1v6m1o-klaus-schwab-why-is-klaus-schwab-a-keynote-speaker-at-the-2022-g20-leaders-.html

»Klaus Schwab stated, "I'm Very Impressed by the Confucian Notion of "Hé Xié." "Hé Xié" in Chinese means to achieve harmony through censorship."

- WATCH - https://rumble.com/v1gp86j-klaus-schwab-klaus-schwab-discusses-the-future-of-censorship-which-he-calls.html

»Klaus Schwab stated, "And of Coarse, China, In The Geo-Political and Geo-Economical Context Plays An Enormous Role."

- WATCH - https://rumble.com/v1h67qp-klaus-schwab-why-did-klaus-schwab-say-we-are-moving-the-world-from-a-unipol.html

»Klaus Schwab stated, "We Have a Great Participation from Business and Governments and At the Moment We Deal with 8 Technologies: Self-Driving Cars, Drones, Artificial Intelligence, Precision Medicine and So On. Now This Approach Is So Attractive That We Now Have the Offer of Governments Like India, China, Japan, Israel, Sweden to Build a Similar Campus In Their Countries."

Visit TimeToFreeAmerica.com/TheHomoDeuce to watch the video clips referenced throughout this book.

- WATCH - https://rumble.com/v1h67jr-klaus-schwab-we-deal-with-eight-technologies-self-driving-cars.html

»Klaus Schwab stated, "The Fourth Industrial Revolution Has Become a Reality. When We Do the Great Reset One of the Most Important Places to Start Will Be to Ensure That the Fruits of the Fourth Industrial Revolution Are Really Shared by All."

- WATCH - https://rumble.com/v1x-9gk6-klaus-schwab-the-fourth-industrial-revolution-has.html

» Klaus Schwab stated, "It Dates Back to 1971. It's Now 600 Highly Educated People Located Around the World Particularly In Geneva Where Our Headquarters Is. The Fourth Industrial Revolution Is Very Disturbing Progress for Many People."

- WATCH - https://rumble.com/v1x9sgw-klaus-schwab-the-history-of-the-world-economic-forum-it-dates-back-to-1971..html

» Klaus Schwab stated, "Now In Order to Be A Winner You Have to Embrace the Fourth Industrial Revolution... Difference of the Fourth Industrial Revolution Is It Doesn't Change What You Are Doing, It Changes You If You Take the Genetic Editing. It's You Who Are Changed."

- WATCH - https://rumble.com/v1x5ghm-klaus-schwab-in-order-to-be-a-winner-you-have-to-embrace-the-fourth-industr.html

Visit TimeToFreeAmerica.com/TheHomoDeuce to watch the video clips referenced throughout this book.

» **Klaus Schwab stated, "If You Look at the Global Economy, the Effect Will Be a Reduction of Purchasing Power. The Economic Restructuring Will Lead to Social Tensions. There Will Be Winners and Losers."**

- *WATCH - https://rumble.com/v1x5jkm-klaus-schwab-if-you-look-at-the-global-economy.html*

» **Klaus Schwab stated "History Is Truly At a Turning Point. We Do Not Yet Know the Full Extent and the Systemic and Structural Changes Which Will Happen. However, We Do Know That Global Energy Systems, Food Systems and Supply Chains Will Be Deeply Affected."**

- *WATCH - https://rumble.com/v1x5ixo-klaus-schwab-history-is-truly-at-a-turning-point..html*

» **Klaus Schwab stated, "We Have to Construct the World of Tomorrow. It's a Systemic Transformation of the World. China Is a Role Model for Many Countries. The Chinese Model Is Certainly a Very Attractive Model for Quite a Number of Countries."**

- *WATCH - https://rumble.com/v1x4kuq-klaus-schwab-we-have-to-construct-the-world-of.htmlhttps://rumble.com/v1x-4kuq-klaus-schwab-we-have-to-construct-the-world-of.html*

Obama & Pastor Rick Warren Attending Davos

Visit TimeToFreeAmerica.com/TheHomoDeuce to watch the video clips referenced throughout this book.

»Klaus Schwab stated, "(The Great Reset) Is Very Disturbing Progress for Many People and They Just Feel Overwhelmed. And This Creates a Tendency for Nationalism…And That Is One of the Reasons for the Success of TRUMP in the United States."

- WATCH - *https://rumble.com/v1xhbmg-klaus-schwab-the-great-rest-is-very-disturbing-progress-for.html*

Visit *TimeToFreeAmerica.com/TheHomoDeuce* to watch
the video clips referenced throughout this book.

90
90

"Science isn't about truth–It's about POWER."

- YUVAL NOAH HARARI

1. WO2020060606 - CRYPTOCURRENCY SYSTEM USING BODY ACTIVITY DATA

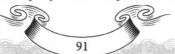

= 666   WØRLD ECONOMIC FORUM   CERN

Visit TimeToFreeAmerica.com/TheHomoDeuce to watch
the video clips referenced throughout this book.

"²And the beast which I saw was like unto a leopard, and his feet were as the feet of a bear, and his mouth as the mouth of a lion: and the dragon gave him his power, and his seat, and great authority."

- REVELATION 13:2 KJV

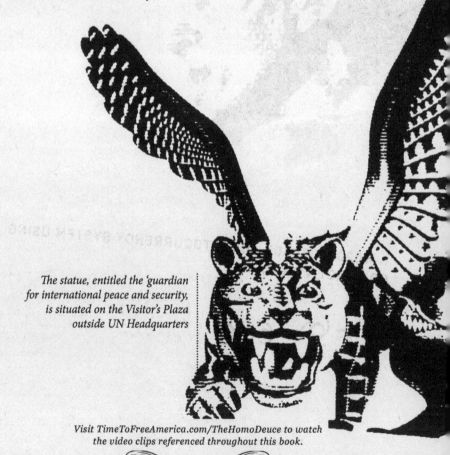

The statue, entitled the 'guardian for international peace and security, is situated on the Visitor's Plaza outside UN Headquarters

Visit *TimeToFreeAmerica.com/TheHomoDeuce* to watch the video clips referenced throughout this book.

CHAPTER 5

60 Biblical Signs of the Times That We Are Living In

#1 - WHY IS THE EUPHRATES RIVER DRYING UP? -

https://www.kingjamesbibleonline.org/Revelation-16-12/

"12 And the sixth angel poured out his vial upon the great river Euphrates; and the water thereof was dried up, that the way of the kings of the east might be prepared. 13 And I saw three unclean spirits like frogs come out of the mouth of the dragon, and out of the mouth of the beast, and out of the mouth of the false prophet. 14 For they are the spirits of devils, working miracles, which go forth unto the kings of the earth and of the whole world, to gather them to the battle of that great day of God Almighty. 15 Behold, I come as a thief. Blessed is he that watcheth, and keepeth his garments, lest he walk naked, and they see his shame. 16 And he gathered them together into a place called in the Hebrew tongue Armageddon."Revelation 16:12-16

Visit TimeToFreeAmerica.com/TheHomoDeuce to watch
the video clips referenced throughout this book.

https://www.thetimes.co.uk/article/iraqs-mighty-rivers-ti-gris-and-euphrates-will-soon-run-dry-q5h72g5sk

WATCH - *https://rumble.com/v1eb6ap-euphrates-river-why-is-the-euphrates-river-drying-up-are-we-witnessing-reve.html*

#2 - WHY DOES MICROSOFT HAVE A PATENT WITH A WO-2020-060606 PUBLICATION NUMBER?

- https://patentscope.wipo.int/search/en/de-tail.jsf?docId=WO202006060

Revelation 13: 16-18 - "16 And he causeth all, both small and great, rich and poor, free and bond, to receive a mark in their right hand, or in their foreheads: 17 And that no man might buy or sell, save he that had the mark, or the name of the beast, or the number of his name. 18 Here is wisdom. Let him that hath understanding count the number of the beast: for it is the number of a man; and his number is Six hundred threescore and six."Revelation 13: 16-18

https://www.biblegateway.com/passage/?search=Rev-elation%2013%3A16-18&version=KJV

> **»Why Did The Gates Foundation Fund This?**
> **"Quantum-dot tattoos hold vaccination record"**

- https://news.rice.edu/news/2019/quan-tum-dot-tattoos-hold-vaccination-record

»Watch - The Great Reset | Yuval Noah Harari "Covid-19 Was the Moment Surveillance Went Under the Skin"

- https://rumble.com/v19kk5c-the-great-re-set-micro-chips-under-your-skin.html

WATCH - *"Central Bank Digital Currency | Freedom-Killing Programmable Currency Explained In 4 Minutes "The Central Bank will have absolute control on the rules and regulations that will determine the use of (currency) that central bank liability."*

https://rumble.com/v1h5zv1-central-bank-digital-curren-cy-freedom-killing-programmable-currency-explain.html

#3 - IS MATTHEW CHAPTER 24 AND LUKE CHAPTER 21 BEING FULFILLED RIGHT IN FRONT OF US?

24 And Jesus went out, and departed from the temple: and his disciples came to him for to shew him the buildings of the temple.

2 And Jesus said unto them, See ye not all these things? verily I say unto you, There shall not be left here one stone upon another, that shall not be thrown down.

Visit TimeToFreeAmerica.com/TheHomoDeuce to watch
the video clips referenced throughout this book.

3 And as he sat upon the mount of Olives, the disciples came unto him privately, saying, Tell us, when shall these things be? and what shall be the sign of thy coming, and of the end of the world?

4 And Jesus answered and said unto them, Take heed that no man <u>deceive you</u>.

....

Watch - Birx Lied | "I Knew These Vaccines Were Never Going to Protect Against Infection."Dr. Deborah Birx - https://rumble.com/v1dczbx-birx-lied-.html

....

Watch - Yuval Noah Harari | "It's Not An Extremely Deadly Virus & Look What It's Doing to the World (Lockdowns)."https://rumble.com/v18f4ya-yuval-noah-harari-its-not-an-extremely-virus-and-look-what-its-doing-to-the.html

....

Watch - The Pope Is Pushing the Climate Emergency | Why Did Yuval Noah Harari Say, "We Have Seen the Current Pope Making Some Very Helpful Statements (About Climate Change)?"- https://rumble.com/v1di2wj-climate-emergency-.html

....

Watch - Climate Emergency | On January 26th 2021, Why Did Senate Majority Leader Chuck Schumer Say "I Think It Would Be a Good Idea for Biden to Call for a Climate Emergency?"https://rumble.com/v1di21r-climate-emergency-.html

....

> **5 For many shall come in my name, saying, I am Christ; and shall deceive many.**

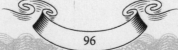

Watch - Why Are mRNA Modifying Nano-Technology Shots Being Pushed On Humanity? Elon Musk | Why Did Elon Musk Say, "We Presume It Would be Consensual Because You Definitely Just Don't Want People Sending Stuff Into Your Brain Without Your Consent?"https://rumble.com/v1eanjn-elon-musk-.html

Watch - Climate Emergency | Why Did Prince Charles Say, "We Have to Reduce the Emissions Urgently. We Need a Vast Military Style Campaign. With TRILLIONS At HIS Disposal Far Beyond Global GDP?"https://rumble.com/v1dhyvj-climate-emergency.html

Watch - Elon Musk | Brain-Computer Interfaces | "There Are People Like Elon Musk Working On Closed Loop Systems." https://rumble.com/v1efchn-elon-musk-brain-computer-interfaces-.html

»6 And ye shall hear of wars and rumors of wars: see that ye be not troubled: for all these things must come to pass, but the end is not yet.

Watch - Ezekiel Chapter 38 Fulfilled? Putin Seeking to Cement Ties With Iran, Turkey in Rare Trip Abroad - https://rumble.com/v1eb4xj-ezekiel-chapter-38-fulfilled-putin-seeking-to-cement-ties-with-iran-turkey-.html

»7 For nation shall rise against nation, and kingdom against kingdom: and there shall be famines, and pestilences, and earthquakes, in diverse places.

WATCH - Climate Emergency | SHOCKING!!! READ The Climate President's Emergency Powers - https://rumble.com/v1di5v7-climate-emergency-.html

Visit TimeToFreeAmerica.com/TheHomoDeuce to watch the video clips referenced throughout this book.

Read - The Truth About America's Food Supply & the Future of Food - https://timetofreeamerica.com/food-shortage/#scroll-content

....

WATCH (Starting At 2:35) - Why a WORLD-WIDE FAMINE Could Be Around the Corner - *https://www.youtube.com/watch?v=4wJH38Iv9pQ*

....

WATCH - Supply Chain Collapse | Diesel Engine Oil OUT-AGE Alert | Supply Chain Wiped Out Until 2023 - Starting At 1:10 - https://rumble.com/v19uia7-supply-chain-collapse-die-sel-engine-oil-outage-alert-supply-chain-wiped-out.html

....

8 All these are the beginning of sorrows. 9 Then shall they deliver you up to be afflicted, and shall kill you: and ye shall be hated of all nations for my name's sake. 10 And then shall many be offended, and shall betray one another, and shall hate one another. 11 And many false prophets shall rise, and shall deceive many. 12 And because iniquity shall abound, the love of many shall wax cold. 13 But he that shall endure unto the end, the same shall be saved. 14 And this gospel of the kingdom shall be preached in all the world for a witness unto all nations; and then shall the end come. 15 When ye therefore shall see the abomination of desolation, spoken of by Daniel the prophet, stand in the holy place, (whoso readeth, let him understand:) 16 Then let them which be in Judaea flee into the mountains: 17 Let him which is on the housetop not come down to take any thing out of his house: 18 Neither let him which is in the field return back to take his clothes. 19 And woe unto them that are with child, and to them that give suck in those days! 20 But pray ye that your flight be not in the winter, neither on the sabbath day: 21 For then shall be great tribulation, such as was not since the beginning of the world to this time, no, nor ever shall

Visit TimeToFreeAmerica.com/TheHomoDeuce to watch
the video clips referenced throughout this book.

98

be. 22 And except those days should be shortened, there should no flesh be saved: but for the elect's sake those days shall be shortened.

WATCH - Why Are "Space Bubbles" Being Pushed by the World Economic Forum to Dim the Sun?
https://senseable.mit.edu/space-bubbles/

Space Bubbles

Read - Luke Chapter 21 - https://www.biblegate-way.com/passage/?search=Luke%2021&version=K-JV#:~:text=21%C2%A0And,to%20hear%20him.

#4 - WHY IS THE WORLD ECONOMIC FORUM LOGO 666? - SEE THE WORLD ECONOMIC FORUM LOGO WWW.WEFORUM.ORG

»How Can the World Not See the Truth?

2 Corinthians 4:4 - "4 In whom the god of this world hath blinded the minds of them which believe not, lest the light of the glorious gospel of Christ, who is the image of God, should shine unto them."

#5 - WHY IS THE CERN LOGO 666? - SEE THEIR LOGO WWW.HOME.CERN

Visit TimeToFreeAmerica.com/TheHomoDeuce to watch the video clips referenced throughout this book.

»"11 And they had a king over them, which is the angel of the bottomless pit, whose name in the Hebrew tongue is Abaddon, but in the Greek tongue hath his name Apollyon."Revelation 9:11

»Revelation 13: 16-18 - "16 And he causeth all, both small and great, rich and poor, free and bond, to receive a mark in their right hand, or in their foreheads:

»17 And that no man might buy or sell, save he that had the mark, or the name of the beast, or the number of his name.

»18 Here is wisdom. Let him that hath understanding count the number of the beast: for it is the number of a man; and his number is Six hundred threescore and six."

WATCH - https://rumble.com/v1b9d3z-cern-why-does-cern-have-a-666-logo.html

#6 - WHY DID CERN NAME THE INTERNET "WWW" WHICH IS "666" IN HEBREW?
RUMBLE.COM/
V1CPML9-666-.HTML

WATCH - The Great Reset | Sign of the Times - https://rumble.com/v1evv7h-the-great-reset-sign-of-the-times.html

Visit TimeToFreeAmerica.com/TheHomoDeuce to watch the video clips referenced throughout this book.

Is the World Wide Web (WWW = 666) the Fulfill-ment of Daniel's Chapter 12 Verse 4 Prophecy?

»**"4 But thou, O Daniel, shut up the words, and seal the book, even to the time of the end: many shall run to and fro, and knowledge shall be increased."Daniel 12:4**

#7 - WHY IS THE WORD CORONA 666?

- *https://www.facebook.com/ieperfest/photos/coro-na-666-oooh-nooofuckcorona-letsbeatcovid19-sociald-istancing-staysafe-metal/10157813796120255/*

#8 - WHY DID BIDEN SIGN TWO-STATE JERUSALEM DECLARATION 666 DAYS AFTER TRUMP SIGNED ABRAHAM ACCORDS?

https://rumble.com/v1cnapl-666-why-did-biden-sign-two-state-jerusalem-declaration-666-days-after-trump.html

»**Two-State Solution | He Just Did It!!! Israeli Prime Minister Yair Lapid Calls for Two-State Israel Solution**

- *WATCH - https://rumble.com/v1l5fsf-two-state-solution-he-just-did-it.html*

Visit TimeToFreeAmerica.com/TheHomoDeuce to watch the video clips referenced throughout this book.

#9 - WHY IS THE GOOGLE CHROME LOGO 666?

- https://www.google.com/search?q=chrome+google+logo+666&-source=lnms&tbm=isch&sa=X&ved=2ahUKEwiX543oxbP6AhXX-lmoFHeDyD4YQ_AUoAXoECAEQAw&biw=1488&bih=781&dpr=1.1

#10 - WHY IS CONGRESS WORKING ON LEGISLATION HR 666?

- Read - *https://www.congress.gov/bill/117th-congress/house-bill/666?q=%7B%22search%22%3A%5B%22A+-bill+to+amend+the+Public+Health+Service+Act+to+provide+-for+public+health+research+and+investment+into+under-standing+and+eliminating+structural+racism+and+po-lice+violence.%22%5D%7D&r=2&s=6*

#11 - WHY IS CONGRESS WORKING ON LEGISLATION HR 6666?

- Read *https://www.congress.gov/bill/116th-con-gress/house-bill/6666/text*

#12 - THE UNITED NATIONS PLACED THE "GUARDIAN OF NATIONS" STATUE IN FRONT

Visit TimeToFreeAmerica.com/TheHomoDeuce to watch the video clips referenced throughout this book.

OF THE UNITED NATIONS BUILDING LOCATED AT 405 EAST 42ND STREET NEW YORK, NEW YORK 10017

**See *https://twitter.com/un_photo/status/1458178013082816513?lang=en*

**Watch - *United Nations "Guardian of Nations" Statue | Why Does the United National Sculpture Look Like the Beast Described In Daniel 7 and Revelation 13?*

https://rumble.com/v1clxtv-united-nations-guardian-of-nations-statue.html

2 And the beast which I saw was like unto a leopard, and his feet were as the feet of a bear, and his mouth as the mouth of a lion: and the dragon gave him his power, and his seat, and great authority."Revelation 13:2

#13 - WHY IS PUTIN SEEKING TO CEMENT TIES WITH IRAN, TURKEY IN RARE TRIP ABROAD?

https://www.wsj.com/articles/putin-seeks-to-cement-ties-with-iran-turkey-in-rare-trip-abroad-11658055769

»**Ezekiel Chapter 38: 1-6**

»**GOG = Prince, Ruler or The Head**

»**Magog = Modern Russian**

Visit TimeToFreeAmerica.com/TheHomoDeuce to watch the video clips referenced throughout this book.

"38 And the word of the Lord came unto me, saying, 2 Son of man, set thy face against Gog, the land of Magog, the chief prince of Meshech and Tubal, and prophesy against him, 3 And say, Thus saith the Lord God; Behold, I am against thee, O Gog, the chief prince of Meshech and Tubal: 4 And I will turn thee back, and put hooks into thy jaws, and I will bring thee forth, and all thine army, horses and horsemen, all of them clothed with all sorts of armor, even a great company with bucklers and shields, all of them handling swords: 5 Persia, Ethiopia, and Libya with them; all of them with shield and helmet: 6 Gomer, and all his bands; the house of Togarmah of the north quarters, and all his bands: and many people with thee." Ezekiel Chapter 38: 1-6

WATCH - Ezekiel Chapter 38 Fulfilled? Putin Seeking to Cement Ties With Iran, Turkey in Rare Trip Abroad - https://rumble.com/v1eb4xj-ezekiel-chapter-38-fulfilled-putin-seeking-to-cement-ties-with-iran-turkey-.html

#14 - WHY IS THE POPE'S AUDIENCE HALL BUILT IN THE SHAPE OF A SNAKE HEAD?

https://en.wikipedia.org/wiki/Paul_VI_Audience_Hall

https://www.google.com/search?q=Paul+VI+Audience+Hall+snake+head&source=lnms&tbm=isch&sa=X-&ved=2ahUKEwjwkrOOxrP6AhV5kWoFHdGEBscQ_AUoAXoECAEQAw&biw=1488&bih=781&dpr=1.1

Visit TimeToFreeAmerica.com/TheHomoDeuce to watch
the video clips referenced throughout this book.

104

#15 - WHY WAS RULES FOR RADICALS WRITTEN BY SAUL ALINSKY AND DEDICATED TO LUCIFER IN 1971?

- https://www.amazon.com/Rules-Radicals-Practical-Primer-Realistic/dp/0679721134

»**READ: "Lest we forget at least an over-the-shoulder acknowledgment to the very first radical: from all our legends, mythology, and history (and who is to know where mythology leaves off and history begins — or which is which), the first radical known to man who rebelled against the establishment and did it so effectively that he at least won his own kingdom — Lucifer."**

- Saul Alinksy - https://thehill.com/blogs/ballot-box/presidential-races/288457-carson-explains-lucifer-comment-clinton-and-alinksy-on-a/

#16 - WHY DID AMERICA START SACRIFICING BABIES TO BAAL IN 1971?

»**"They have also built the high places of Baal, to burn their sons with fire for burnt offerings unto Baal, which I commanded not nor spoke it, neither came it into My mind."Jeremiah 19:5**

WATCH - *Kanye 'Ye' West | "The Most Dangerous Place for a Black Person In America Is In Their Mother's Stomach. The Abortion Clinics Were Created by Eugenicists for Population Control and It's Controlling the Population."https://rumble.com/v1q5fhd-kanye-ye-west-the-most-dangerous-place-for-a-black-person-in-america-is-in.html*

#17 - WHY DID KLAUS SCHWAB START THE WORLD ECONOMIC FORUM IN 1971?

WATCH - *WORLD PREMIER | Explosive Documentary "1971: THE YEAR THE WORLD GOT THE SHAFT"https://rumble.com/v117zct-world-premier-explosive-documentary-1971-the-year-the-world-got-the-shaft.html*

#18 - WHY DID AMERICA GET OFF OF THE GOLD STANDARD IN 1971?

"The silver is mine, and the gold is mine, saith the LORD of hosts."Haggai 2:8

»**Countries That Have Moved Off of the U.S. Dollar: Brazil, Russia, China, India, Saudi Arabia, Zimbabwe, and Iran.**

WATCH - *BRICS | As Saudi Arabia Joins BRICS Can BRICS De-Dollarize the Global Financial System? What Will Happen to the U.S. Dollar? - https://rumble.com/v1q8lbp-brics-as-saudi-arabia-joins-brics-can-brics.html*

Visit TimeToFreeAmerica.com/TheHomoDeuce to watch the video clips referenced throughout this book.

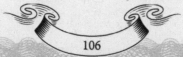

#19 - WHY DOES YUVAL NOAH HARARI WANT TO CHANGE THE LAWS?

READ - *"And he shall speak great words against the most High, and shall wear out the saints of the most High, and think to change times and laws: and they shall be given into his hand until a time and times and the dividing of time." Daniel 7:25*
- https://www.kingjamesbibleonline.org/Daniel-7-25/

»**What is the Anthropocene? And why does it matter?**

- https://www.weforum.org/agenda/2016/08/what-is-the-anthropocene-and-why-does-it-matter/

WATCH - *Yuval Noah Harari | Yuval Advocates Changing the Legal System | "The Idea That We Punish People for Making Bad Choices That Should Be Out."https:// rumble.com/v1c8mhr-yuval-noah-harari-.html*

#20 - WHY IS YUVAL NOAH HARARI WANTING TO CHANGE THE TIMES?

"And he shall speak great words against the most High, and shall wear out the saints of the most High, and think to change times and laws: and they shall be given into his hand until a time and times and the dividing of time."Daniel 7:25

Visit TimeToFreeAmerica.com/TheHomoDeuce to watch the video clips referenced throughout this book.

WATCH - The Anthropocene | Why Did Yuval Noah Hara-ri Say. "For the Elite It Will Work. When the Flood Comes, the Scientists Will Build a Noah's Ark for the Elite, Leaving the Rest of the People to Drown?"- https://rumble.com/v1eav6x-the-anthropocene-why-did-yuval-noah-harari-say.html

» **What is the Anthropocene? And why does it matter? -**

https://www.weforum.org/agenda/2016/08/what-is-the-anthropocene-and-why-does-it-matter/

#21 - WHY ARE YUVAL NOAH HARARI, KLAUS SCHWAB AND ELON MUSK DISCUSSING CONNECTING BRAINS TO COMPUTERS?

"These have one mind, and shall give their power and strength unto the beast." Revelation 17:13

WATCH - Yuval Noah Harari | "Once You Can Connect Brains and Computers...You Can Connect Several Brains Together." https://rumble.com/v1cff61-yuval-noah-harari-once-you-can-connect-brains-and-computers....html

» **WATCH - Ray Kurzweil | "We Will Connect Wirelessly Our Neocortex to the Cloud (with Nanobots That Enter Your Neocortex)"**

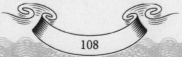

- https://rumble.com/v1q5tq3-ray-kurzweil-we-will-con-nect-wirelessly-our-neocortex-to-the-cloud.html

....

WATCH - Elon Musk | Why Is Elon Musk Talking About "Writing to the Brain?"https://rumble.com/v1eatkv-elon-musk-why-is-elon-musk-talking-about-writing-to-the-brain.html

....

WATCH - Elon Musk | Why Did Elon Musk Say, "We Could Actually Send the True Thoughts Uncompressed to Some-body Else?"https://rumble.com/v1eatrt-elon-musk.html

....

WATCH - Elon Musk | "This Is Increasingly Sound-ing Like a BLACK MIRROR Episode. You Could Store Your Memories As a Backup and Download Them Into a New Body."https://rumble.com/v1easph-elon-musk-.html

....

WATCH - Yuval Noah Harari | Creating a One World Government / Global Health Care System | "Ideally the Response to COVID Should Be the Creation of a Global Health Care System."Watch - https://rumble.com/v1c8obv-yuval-noah-harari.html

....

#22 - WHY DOES YUVAL NOAH HARARI KEEP REFERRING TO THE ELITE BUILDING A NOAH'S ARK LEAVING THE REST OF HUMANITY TO DROWN?

"37 <u>But as the days of Noah were, so shall also the coming of the Son of man be</u>. 38 For as in the days that were before the flood they were eating and drinking, marrying and giving in marriage, until the day that Noah entered into the ark, 39 And knew not until the flood came, and took them all away; so shall also the coming of the Son of man be."Matthew Chapter 24: 37-39

....

Visit TimeToFreeAmerica.com/TheHomoDeuce to watch
the video clips referenced throughout this book.

109

WATCH - *The Anthropocene | Why Did Yuval Noah Harari Say. "For the Elite It Will Work. When the Flood Comes, the Scientists Will Build a Noah's Ark for the Elite, Leaving the Rest of the People to Drown?"WATCH -* https://rumble.com/v1eav6x-the-anthropocene-why-did-yuval-noah-harari-say.html

#23 - WHAT DOES YUVAL NOAH HARARI MEAN?

What Does Yuval Mean?

»FACT: Yuval is a Hebrew first name. It means "father of music," stream, brook, or tributary. In the Hebrew Bible, Yuval (also Jubal) was the son of Lamech and Adah, a brother of Jabal, a descendant of Cain. He was named as the ancestor of all who played the lyre and pipe (see book of Genesis 4:20-21). A descendant of Cain, his father is Lamech and his brother is Jabal.

"19 And Lamech took unto him two wives: the name of the one was Adah, and the name of the other Zillah. 20 And Adah bare Jabal: he was the father of such as dwell in tents, and of such as have cattle. 21 And his brother's name was Jubal: he was the father of all such as handle the harp and organ."Genesis 4: 19-22

»**Prior to Satan's Fall Was Satan In Charge of the Music In Heaven?**

Visit TimeToFreeAmerica.com/TheHomoDeuce to watch
the video clips referenced throughout this book.

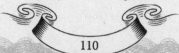

110

Ezekial Chapter 28: 14-18 - "14 Thou art the anointed cherub that covereth; and I have set thee so: thou wast upon the holy mountain of God; thou hast walked up and down in the midst of the stones of fire. 15 Thou wast perfect in thy ways from the day that thou wast created, till iniquity was found in thee. 16 By the multitude of thy merchandise they have filled the midst of thee with violence, and thou hast sinned: therefore I will cast thee as profane out of the mountain of God: and I will destroy thee, O covering cherub, from the midst of the stones of fire. 17 Thine heart was lifted up because of thy beauty, thou hast corrupted thy wisdom by reason of thy brightness: I will cast thee to the ground, I will lay thee before kings, that they may behold thee. 18 Thou hast defiled thy sanctuaries by the multitude of thine iniquities, by the iniquity of thy traffick; therefore will I bring forth a fire from the midst of thee, it shall devour thee, and I will bring thee to ashes upon the earth in the sight of all them that behold thee."

What Does Harari Mean?

> **»FACT: Harari is a Jewish surname that can be translated from Hebrew as 'mountainous' or as 'mountain dweller."**

"12 How art thou fallen from heaven, O Lucifer, son of the morning! how art thou cut down to the ground, which didst weaken the nations! 13 For thou hast said in thine heart, I will ascend into heaven, I will exalt my throne above the stars of God: I will sit also upon the mount of the congregation, in the sides of the north: 14 I will ascend above the heights of the clouds; I will be like the most High. 15 Yet thou shalt be brought down to hell, to the sides of the pit."Isaiah 14: 12-15

WATCH - Yuval Noah Harari | "Scientists Will Build a No-ah's Ark for ELITE Leaving the Rest to Drown."https://rumble.com/v19iy5n-yuval-noah-harari-scientists-will-build-a-noahs-ark-for-elite-leaving-the-r.html

#24- WHY DOES THE UNITED NATIONS HAVE A STATUE IN FRONT OF IT THAT LOOKS LIKE THE EXACT PHYSICAL EMBODIMENT OF REVELATION 13:2?

"And the beast which I saw was like unto a leopard, and his feet were as the feet of a bear, and his mouth as the mouth of a lion: and the dragon gave him his power, and his seat, and great authority."Revelation 13:2

WATCH - United Nations "Guardian of Nations" Statue | Why Does the United National Sculpture Look Like the Beast Described In Daniel 7 and Revelation 13? - https://rumble.com/v1clxtv-united-nations-guardian-of-nations-statue.html

#25 - WHY IS CHINA OPENLY DISCUSSING ADDING WINGS TO THE TIGER?

"And the beast which I saw was like unto a leopard, and his feet were as the feet of a bear, and his mouth as the mouth of a lion: and the dragon gave him his power, and his seat, and great authority."Revelation 13:2

Visit TimeToFreeAmerica.com/TheHomoDeuce to watch the video clips referenced throughout this book.

Watch - Why Is China Openly Discussing Adding Wings to the Tiger? - https://rumble.com/v11ulmc-klaus-schwab-adding-wings-to-tiger-the-great-reset.html

Watch - The United Nations placed the "Guardian of Nations" statue in front of the United Nations building located at 405 East 42nd Street New York, New York 10017. https://twitter.com/un_photo/status/1458178013082816513?lang=en

#26 - THE ANTI-CHRIST PROPHET WILL WANT TO BAN THE EATING OF MEAT:

"4 Now the Spirit speaketh expressly, that in the latter times some shall depart from the faith, giving heed to seducing spirits, and doctrines of devils; 2 Speaking lies in hypocrisy; having their conscience seared with a hot iron; 3 Forbidding to marry, and commanding to abstain from meats, which God hath created to be received with thanksgiving of them which believe and know the truth." 1st Timothy 4:1-3

WATCH - Why Does the POPE Tell Young People "Eating Meat Is Part of a Self-Destructive Trend?"https://rumble.com/v1dls7r-climate-emergency-.html

Visit TimeToFreeAmerica.com/TheHomoDeuce to watch
the video clips referenced throughout this book.

113

WATCH - Costume Ideas | Last Minute Costume Ideas for Andy "Not Manly" Stanley, TD "Fakes" Jakes and "Slick" Rick Warren - <u>https://rumble.com/v1q7in5-costume-ideas-last-minute-costume-ideas-for-andy-not-manly-stanley-td-fakes.html</u>

#27 - THE ANTI-CHRIST PROPHET WILL WANT TO TURN HIMSELF INTO GOD AND TO CREATE HIS OWN RELIGION: "HE WILL NOT BELIEVE IN ANY GOD AT ALL (EXCEPT FOR HIMSELF)."DANIEL 11:37

WATCH - Yuval Noah Harari | "Data-ism Is the Idea w/ Enough Data..You Can Control & Manipulate This Person." <u>https://rumble.com/v1a02pe-yuval-noah-harari-data-ism-is-the-idea-w-enough-data..you-can-control-and-m.html</u>

#28 - WHY DOES YUVAL NOAH HARARI HAVE NO DESIRE FOR WOMEN? "NEITHER SHALL HE REGARD THE GOD OF HIS FATHERS, NOR THE DESIRE OF WOMEN, NOR REGARD ANY GOD: FOR HE SHALL MAGNIFY HIMSELF ABOVE ALL."DANIEL 11:37

Visit TimeToFreeAmerica.com/TheHomoDeuce to watch
the video clips referenced throughout this book.

114

WATCH - Yuval Noah Harari | "The Clear Cut Dichotomy of Men and Women Will No Longer Make Any Sense." [https:// rumble.com/v1cakfr-yuval-noah-harari-the-clear-cut-di-chotomy-of-men-and-women-will-no-longer-m.html](https://rumble.com/v1cakfr-yuval-noah-harari-the-clear-cut-dichotomy-of-men-and-women-will-no-longer-m.html)

"He will have "no regard for the desire of women": He will either be asexual or homosexual"Daniel 11:37

#29 - WHY IS YUVAL NOAH HARARI ADVOCATING FOR THE ENDING OF CLEAR-CUT GENDERS?

"He will seek to forbid marriage and will command people to abstain from eating meat." 1 Timothy 4:3 - [https:// rumble.com/v1camvl-yuval-noah-harari.html](https://rumble.com/v1camvl-yuval-noah-harari.html)

WATCH - Yuval Noah Harari | "The Clear Cut Dichotomy of Men and Women Will No Longer Make Any Sense."[https:// rumble.com/v1cakfr-yuval-noah-harari-the-clear-cut-di-chotomy-of-men-and-women-will-no-longer-m.html](https://rumble.com/v1cakfr-yuval-noah-harari-the-clear-cut-dichotomy-of-men-and-women-will-no-longer-m.html)

#30 - WHY ARE BILL GATES AND KLAUS SCHWAB WANTING TO DIM THE SUN AND TO SHORTEN THE DAYS?

Visit TimeToFreeAmerica.com/TheHomoDeuce to watch the video clips referenced throughout this book.

"22 And except those days should be shortened, there should no flesh be saved: but for the elect's sake those days shall be shortened. 23 Then if any man shall say unto you, Lo, here is Christ, or there; believe it not. 24 For there shall arise false Christs, and false prophets, and shall shew great signs and wonders; insomuch that, if it were possible, they shall deceive the very elect."Matthew 24:22-24

WATCH - Climate Emergency | "Bill Gates Is Creating a Massive Chemical Cloud That Could Cool the Earth." https://rumble.com/v1djg0d-climate-emergency-bill-gates-is-creating-a-massive-chemical-cloud-that-coul.html

WATCH - Climate Emergency | "World Economic Forum Pushes SPACE BUBBLES to Block Out the Sun and to Stop Climate Change"https://rumble.com/v1djf6n-climate-emergency-.html

»Bill Gates | Space Bubbles? | Why Is Bill Gates Trying to Block Out the Sun's Rays with Solar GEO Engineering and Space Bubbles?

- WATCH - https://rumble.com/v1qbjwv-bill-gates-space-bubbles-why-is-bill-gates-trying-to-block-out-the-suns-ray.html

READ - Why Are "Space Bubbles" Being Pushed by the World Economic Forum to Dim the Sun? https://senseable.mit.edu/space-bubbles/

#31 - WHY DOES YUVAL NOAH HARARI OBSESS ABOUT UPGRADING HUMANS INTO GODS? "HE WILL

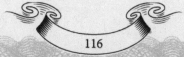

CLAIM TO BE GREATER THAN
ANY GOD."DANIEL 11:37

WATCH - Yuval Noah Harari | "What Kinds of gods Will We Be? Petty, Vengeful and Irresponsible gods?"https://rumble.com/v1a022f-yuval-noah-harari-what-kinds-of-gods-will-we-be-petty-vengefully-and-irresp.html

....

WATCH - Yuval Noah Harari | "We May Be Facing a New Kind of Inequality. The Upgrade Elite of Super Humans and a New Massive Useless Class."https://rumble.com/v1b34x5-yuval-noah-harari-we-may-be-facing-a-new-kind-of-inequality....html

....

WATCH - Yuval Noah Harari | "We Will Become Gods, But We Will Be Dissatisfied Gods." https://rumble.com/v10xwa6-yuval-noah-harari-we-will-become-gods-but-we-will-be-dissatisfied-gods..html

....

WATCH - Yuval Noah Harari | WEF Lead Advisor, "We Are Now Basically the Gods of Planet Earth."https://rumble.com/v11bb6c-yuval-noah-harari-wef-lead-advisor-we-are-now-basically-the-gods-of-planet-.html

....

WATCH - Yuval Noah Harari | "Upgrading Humans Into Gods," & "Shifting Authority from Humans to Algorithms"https://rumble.com/v10amed-yuval-noah-harari-upgrading-humans-into-gods-and-shifting-authority-from-hu.html

....

Visit TimeToFreeAmerica.com/TheHomoDeuce to watch
the video clips referenced throughout this book.

117

#32 - WHY IS YUVAL NOAH HARARI PUSHING FOR THE CREATION OF A SYSTEM WHERE YOU CAN'T BUY OR SELL WITH TECHNOLOGY GOING UNDER YOUR SKIN?

Revelation 13: 16-18 - "16 And he causeth all, both small and great, rich and poor, free and bond, to receive a mark in their right hand, or in their foreheads: 17 And that no man might buy or sell, save he that had the mark, or the name of the beast, or the number of his name. 18 Here is wisdom. Let him that hath understanding count the number of the beast: for it is the number of a man; and his number is Six hundred threescore and six." Revelation 13: 16-18

https://www.biblegateway.com/passage/?search=Revelation%2013%3A16-18&version=KJV

....

WATCH - *The Great Reset | Yuval Noah Harari "Covid-19 Was the Moment Surveillance Went Under the Skin"* https://rumble.com/v19kk5c-the-great-reset-micro-chips-under-your-skin.html

....

#33 - WHY IS THE WORLD ECONOMIC FORUM PUSHING FOR MICROCHIPS TO BE IMPLANTED UNDER YOUR SKIN?

16 And he causeth all, both small and great, rich and poor, free and bond, to receive a mark in their right hand, or in their foreheads: 17 And that no man might buy or sell, save he that had the mark, or the name of the beast, or the number of his name. 18 Here is wisdom. Let him that hath understanding count the

number of the beast: for it is the number of a man; and his number is Six hundred threescore and six."*Revelation 13: 16-18*

WATCH - The Great Reset | *"Microchips to Implant Under Your Skin. Most Likely Implanted In Your Hand."*https://rumble.com/v10y221-the-great-reset-microchips-to-implant-under-your-skin.-most-likely-implante.html

WATCH - Yuval Noah Harari | *"Your Immune Systems Will Be Connected to the Net."*https://rumble.com/v1c9dt1-yuval-noah-harari-your-immune-systems-will-be-connected-to-net.html

#34 - WHY ARE THE BUSINESS LEADERS OF THE WORLD ALL BEING DECEIVED INTO PUSHING MRNA MODIFYING NANO TECHNOLOGY TO BE INJECTED INTO HUMANS THAT HAVE THE ABILITY TO CONTROL THEIR THOUGHTS?

Revelation 18:23 - "And the light of a candle shall shine no more at all in thee; and the voice of the bridegroom and of the bride shall be heard no more at all in thee: for thy merchants were the great men of the earth; for by thy sorceries were all nations deceived."

WATCH - Doctor Robert Malone | *Did Dr. Malone Say, "mRNA Technology Is the Entry Point to Transhumanism?"* https://rumble.com/v1abn23-robert-malone-mrna-technology-is-the-entry-point-to-transhumanism.html

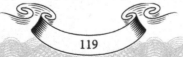

*WATCH - Klaus Schwab | "We Deal with 8 Technologies: Self-Driving Cars, Drones, Artificial Intelligence, Precision Medicine, etc. We Now Have the Offer of Governments Like India, China, Japan, Israel and Sweden"*https://rumble.com/v1eb9zf-klaus-schwab.html

WATCH - BREAKING!!! General Flynn | Why Is China Developing Mind-Controlling Weapons Via Gene-Editing? - https://rumble.com/vrk3ax-breaking-general-flynn-why-is-china-developing-mind-controlling-weapons-via.html

WATCH - Transhumanism | "By 2030 Smartphones Will Be Built Into Bodies."Pekka Lundmark (Nokia CEO) - https://rumble.com/v16plao-transhumanism-by-2030-smartphones-will-be-built-into-bodies.-pekka-lundmark.html

#35 - WHY DOES YUVAL NOAH HARARI CLAIM THAT HE CAN BECOME GOD? 2 THESSALONIANS 2:4 - "HE WILL CLAIM TO BE GOD."

*WATCH - Yuval Noah Harari | "What Kinds of gods Will We Be? Petty, Vengefully and Irresponsible gods?"*https://rumble.com/v1ao22f-yuval-noah-harari-what-kinds-of-gods-will-we-be-petty-vengefully-and-irresp.html

Visit TimeToFreeAmerica.com/TheHomoDeuce to watch
the video clips referenced throughout this book.

120

WATCH - Yuval Noah Harari | "God Is Dead It Just Takes Awhile to Get Rid of the Body." Says WEF Advisor " https://rumble.com/v10d400-yuval-noah-harari-god-is-dead-it-just-takes-awhile-to-get-rid-of-the-body.-.html

WATCH - Yuval Noah Harari | Why Is Yuval Recommending "Anti Viruses for the Brain" and "New Religions" Offering Eternal Life On Earth? https://rumble.com/v1c4l3v-yuval-noah-harari-anti-viruses-for-the-brain-new-religions-and-eternal-life.html

#36 - WHY IS YUVAL NOAH HARARI OBSESSED WITH DISCOURAGING MARRIAGE AND THE EATING OF MEAT?

"He will seek to forbid marriage and will command people to abstain from eating meat." 1 Timothy 4:3 - https://rumble.com/v1camvl-yuval-noah-harari.html

WATCH - Yuval Noah Harari | MEAT | "I Refrain from Eating Meat to Prolong the Life of the Chickens and Cows." https://rumble.com/v1cdvnh-yuval-noah-harari-i-refrain-from-eating-meat-to-prolong-the-life-of-the-chi.html

WATCH - Yuval Noah Harari | MEAT | "Is It Ok to Inflict Pain On Cows to Provide Pleasure for Human Beings." https://rumble.com/v1cduxl-yuval-noah-harari-meat-is-it-ok-to-inflict-pain-on-cows-to-provide-pleasure.html

Visit TimeToFreeAmerica.com/TheHomoDeuce to watch the video clips referenced throughout this book.

WATCH - *Yuval Noah Harari | "What to Do With Useless People? My Recommendation Is Drugs & Computer Games."*https://rumble.com/v1oah9d-yuval-noah-harari-what-to-do-with-useless-people-my-recommendation-is-drugs.html

WATCH - *Yuval Noah Harari | "You Don't Need Children, You Can Have a Pension Fund. You Don't Need Neighbors, Sisters or Brothers. The State Provides You With Everything."*https://rumble.com/v1ch7et-yuval-noah-harari-.html

#37 - WHY ARE MANY MAINSTREAM PASTORS AND THE POPE PUSHING COVID-19 / THE GREAT RESET AGENDA?

"4 I charge thee therefore before God, and the Lord Jesus Christ, who shall judge the quick and the dead at his appearing and his kingdom; 2 Preach the word; be instant in season, out of season; reprove, rebuke, exhort with all long suffering and doctrine. 3 For the time will come when they will not endure sound doctrine; but after their own lusts shall they heap to themselves teachers, having itching ears; 4 And they shall turn away their ears from the truth, and shall be turned unto fables."

2nd Timothy 4:1-4

WATCH - *Andy Stanley | Why Did Andy Stanley Say, "We Have to Go to the Grocery Store, We Have to Go to Work, But We Don't Have to Go to Church?"*https://rumble.com/v1elxdd-andy-stanley-.html

Visit TimeToFreeAmerica.com/TheHomoDeuce to watch
the video clips referenced throughout this book.

WATCH - TD Jakes | Why Did TD Jakes Team Promote Anthony Fauci and the COVID-19 Vaccines? - https://rumble.com/v1elx03-td-jakes-why-did-td-jakes-team-promote-anthony-fauci-and-the-covid-19-vacci.html

WATCH - Rick Warren | "Francis Collins and I Have Been Friends for Many Years. We Met When We Were Both Speaking at the World Economic Forum."https://rumble.com/v1eluf1-rick-warren-.html

WATCH - Rick Warren | "I'm Here At (The World Economic Forum) Davos Here with My Friends."https://rumble.com/v1elv2x-rick-warren-im-here-at-the-world-economic-forum-davos-here-with-my-friends..html

WATCH - Klaus Schwab | "If I Look At Our Stakeholders. We Have Partnerships with Many Very Important Scientists, Academia, Media and Religious Leaders."https://rumble.com/v1elwef-klaus-schwab-.html

WATCH - Rick Warren | "Local Churches Have Credibility. You Have to Have the Faith Sector, the Public Sector and the Private Sector."https://rumble.com/v1elwhh-rick-warren-.html

#38 - PALESTINIANS TO DISCUSS FULL RECOGNITION OF 'STATE OF PALESTINE' IN UPCOMING U.N. SESSION WITH JOE BIDEN -

Visit TimeToFreeAmerica.com/TheHomoDeuce to watch the video clips referenced throughout this book.

READ - *https://www.breitbart.com/middle-east/2022/08/12/palestinians-discuss-full-recognition-of-state-of-palestine-in-upcoming-un-session-with-biden/*

···

READ - 77th Session of the UN General Assembly (UNGA 77) - https://sdg.iisd.org/events/77th-session-of-the-un-general-assembly-unga-77/#:~:text=The%2077th%20session%20of%20the,be%20Tuesday%2C%2020%20September%202022.

···

Joel 3:2 - "2 I will also gather all nations, and will bring them down into the valley of Jehoshaphat, and will plead with them there for my people and for my heritage Israel, whom they have scattered among the nations, and parted my land."

···

Zechariah 12: 1-3 "1 The burden of the word of the Lord for Israel, saith the Lord, which stretcheth forth the heavens, and layeth the foundation of the earth, and formeth the spirit of man within him. 2 Behold, I will make Jerusalem a cup of trembling unto all the people round about, when they shall be in the siege both against Judah and against Jerusalem. 3 And in that day will I make Jerusalem a burdensome stone for all people: all that burden themselves with it shall be cut in pieces, though all the people of the earth be gathered together against it."

···

#39 - WHY IS THE POPE PERPETUATING THE CLIMATE CHANGE NARRATIVE?

»Why Is the Pope Encouraging People to Abstain from the Eating of Meat?

Visit TimeToFreeAmerica.com/TheHomoDeuce to watch the video clips referenced throughout this book.

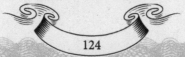

»Why Is Rick Warren Celebrating Francis Collins and the World Economic Forum?

»Why Is TD Jakes Teaming Up with Anthony Fauci to Encourage His World-Wide Audience to Put RNA-Modifying Nano-Technology Inside of Their Bodies?

»Why Is Andy Stanley Encouraging People to Not Go to Church?

»Why Is Dante Bowe Celebrating the Music of the Satanic Artist Lil Nas X? -

2nd Thessalonians Chapter 2:1-4 - "2 Now we beseech you, brethren, by the coming of our Lord Jesus Christ, and by our gathering together unto him, 2 That ye be not soon shaken in mind, or be troubled, neither by spirit, nor by word, nor by letter as from us, as that the day of Christ is at hand. 3 <u>Let no man deceive you by any means: for that day shall not come, except there come a falling away first, and that man of sin be revealed, the son of perdition;</u> 4 Who opposeth and exalteth himself above all that is called God, or that is worshiped; so that he as God sitteth in the temple of God, shewing himself that he is God.

READ - The evangelical church faces a 'state of emergency' over the pandemic and politics, Andy Stanley says - https://www.cnn.com/2022/06/04/us/andy-stanley-evangelicals-book-blake-cec/index.html

WATCH - Klaus Schwab | "If I Look At Our Stakeholders. We Have Partnerships with Many Very Important Scientists, Academia, Media and Religious Leaders."https://rumble.com/v1elwef-klaus-schwab-.html

Visit TimeToFreeAmerica.com/TheHomoDeuce to watch the video clips referenced throughout this book.

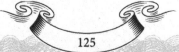

WATCH - Rick Warren | "Local Churches Have Credibility. You Have to Have the Faith Sector, the Public Sector and the Private Sector."https://rumble.com/v1elwhh-rick-warren-.html

WATCH - Climate Emergency | Why Did Yuval Noah Harari Say, "We Have Seen the Current Pope Making Some Very Helpful Statements (About Climate Change)?"https:// rumble.com/v1di2wj-climate-emergency-.html

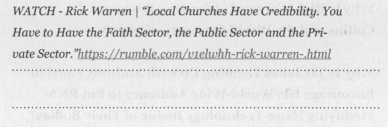

»**Why Is "Christian-Artist" Dante Bowe Most Looking Forward to Watching Lil Nas X Perform? - https:// rumble.com/v1ol5iw-why-is-christian-artist-dante-bowe-most-looking-forward-to-watching-lil-nas.html**

Learn More About Evangelist Joe Morris Today At: www.JosephMorris.com

#40 - WHY IS IT SIGNIFICANT THAT ISRAEL REGATHERED IN 1948?

"37 Thus saith the Lord God; I will yet for this be enquired of by the house of Israel, to do it for them; I will increase them with men like a flock. 38 As the holy flock, as the flock of Jerusalem in her solemn feasts; so shall the waste cities be filled with flocks of men: and they shall know that I am the Lord." Ezekiel 36:37-38

https://www.biblegateway.com/passage/?-search=Ezekiel%2036%3A37-38&version=KJV

Visit TimeToFreeAmerica.com/TheHomoDeuce to watch
the video clips referenced throughout this book.

Matthew Chapter 24: 27-37

"27 For as the lightning cometh out of the east, and shineth even unto the west; so shall also the coming of the Son of man be. 28 For wheresoever the carcase is, there will the eagles be gathered together. 29 Immediately after the tribulation of those days shall the sun be darkened, and the moon shall not give her light, and the stars shall fall from heaven, and the powers of the heavens shall be shaken: 30 And then shall appear the sign of the Son of man in heaven: and then shall all the tribes of the earth mourn, and they shall see the Son of man coming in the clouds of heaven with power and great glory. 31 And he shall send his angels with a great sound of a trumpet, and they shall gather together his elect from the four winds, from one end of heaven to the other. 32 Now learn a parable of the fig tree; When his branch is yet tender, and putteth forth leaves, ye know that summer is nigh: 33 So likewise ye, when ye shall see all these things, know that it is near, even at the doors. 34 Verily I say unto you, This generation shall not pass, till all these things be fulfilled. 35 Heaven and earth shall pass away, but my words shall not pass away. 36 But of that day and hour knoweth no man, no, not the angels of heaven, but my Father only. 37 But as the days of Noah were, so shall also the coming of the Son of man be."

Luke 21: 20-38

"20 And when ye shall see Jerusalem compassed with armies, then know that the desolation thereof is nigh. 21 Then let them which are in Judaea flee to the mountains; and let them which are in the midst of it depart out; and let not them that are in the countries enter thereinto. 22 For these be the days of vengeance, that all things which are written may be fulfilled. 23 But woe unto them that are with child, and to them that give suck, in those days! for there shall be great distress in the land, and wrath upon this people. 24 And they shall

Visit TimeToFreeAmerica.com/TheHomoDeuce to watch
the video clips referenced throughout this book.

fall by the edge of the sword, and shall be led away captive into all nations: and Jerusalem shall be trodden down of the Gentiles, until the times of the Gentiles be fulfilled. 25 And there shall be signs in the sun, and in the moon, and in the stars; and upon the earth distress of nations, with perplexity; the sea and the waves roaring; 26 Men's hearts failing them for fear, and for looking after those things which are coming on the earth: for the powers of heaven shall be shaken. 27 And then shall they see the Son of man coming in a cloud with power and great glory. 28 And when these things begin to come to pass, then look up, and lift up your heads; for your redemption draweth nigh. 29 And he spake to them a parable; Behold the fig tree, and all the trees; 30 When they now shoot forth, ye see and know of your own selves that summer is now nigh at hand. 31 So likewise yé, when ye see these things come to pass, know ye that the kingdom of God is nigh at hand. 32 Verily I say unto you, This generation shall not pass away, till all be fulfilled. 33 Heaven and earth shall pass away: but my words shall not pass away. 34 And take heed to yourselves, lest at any time your hearts be overcharged with surfeiting, and drunkenness, and cares of this life, and so that day come upon you unawares. 35 For as a snare shall it come on all them that dwell on the face of the whole earth. 36 Watch ye therefore, and pray always, that ye may be accounted worthy to escape all these things that shall come to pass, and to stand before the Son of man. 37 And in the day time he was teaching in the temple; and at night he went out, and abode in the mount that is called the mount of Olives. 38 And all the people came early in the morning to him in the temple, for to hear him."

Visit TimeToFreeAmerica.com/TheHomoDeuce to watch the video clips referenced throughout this book.

#41 - WHY IS IT SIGNIFICANT THAT JERUSALEM WAS REGATHERED IN 1967?

"24 And they shall fall by the edge of the sword, and shall be led away captive into all nations: and Jerusalem shall be trodden down of the Gentiles, until the times of the Gentiles be fulfilled."Luke 21: 24

#42 - WHY DOES THE EUROPEAN UNION'S MONEY HAVE THE WOMAN FROM THE BOOK OF REVELATION ON IT?

https://www.google.com/search?q=european+union+money+revelation&tbm=isch&ved=2ahUKEwjEkuvF_d35AhXbgokEHdyZCwcQ2-cCegQIABAA&oq=european+union+money+revelation&gs_lcp=CgNpbWcQAzoECAAQQzoECAAQGD0E-CAAQHlCLB1jBHmDgH2gCcAB4AIABR4gBqwaSAQIxNJgBAK-ABAaoBC2d3cy13aXotaW1nwAEB&sclient=img&ei=k1AFY4T-9DtuFptQP3LOuOA&bih=760&biw=1314#imgrc=ag5jy9l1P0Pu8M

Revelation 17: https://www.biblegateway.com/passage/?search=Revelation%2017&version=KJV

#43 - WHY DOES THE TOWER OF BABEL LOOK EXACTLY LIKE THE EU CAPITAL BUILDING IN FRANCE?

- https://www.google.com/search?q=EU+Capital+Building+France+tower+of+babel&sxsrf=ALiCzsY4kl3DEj502m-wAf8BHv6N-p_d43A:1661292777092&source=lnms&tbm=isch&sa=X&ved=2ahUKEwj8seLu_d35AhUmmWoFHb4lDX-MQ_AUoAXoECAEQAw&cshid=1661292807584270&biw=1314&bih=760&dpr=1.1#imgrc=fEl8BvDiBBT1uM

Read: https://www.europarl.europa.eu/news/en/faq/19/why-was-strasbourg-designated-the-official-seat-of-the-european-parliament

#44 - WHY IS IT SIGNIFICANT THAT FOXES SEEN WALKING NEAR THE WESTERN WALL & FULFILLING BIBLICAL PROMISE?

- https://www.jpost.com/israel-news/foxes-seen-walking-near-the-western-wall-fulfilling-biblical-promise-598053

Lamentations 5:18 - "18 Because of the mountain of Zion, which is desolate, the foxes walk upon it." https://www.biblegateway.com/passage/?search=Lamentations%205%3A18&version=KJV

#45 - WHY IS IT SIGNIFICANT THAT THE DEAD SEA COMING BACK TO LIFE; FISH SEEN SWIMMING ON THE SHORES?

https://www.christiantoday.com/article/bible-prophecy-being-fulfilled-dead-sea-coming-back-to-life-fish-seen-swimming-on-the-shores/91895.htm

"And it shall come to pass, that every thing that liveth, which moveth, whithersoever the rivers shall come, shall live: and there shall be a very great multitude of fish, because these waters shall come thither: for they shall be healed; and everything shall live whither the river cometh."Ezekiel 47:9

#46 - WHY IS THE DEAD SEA TURNING BLOOD RED? - DEAD SEA POOL TURNS BLOOD RED PUZZLING EXPERTS IN REGION WHERE THE BIBLE SAYS GOD SENT ANGELS TO DESTROY SODOM AND GOMORRAH FOR THEIR INHABITANTS' SINS -

https://www.dailymail.co.uk/news/article-9985759/Dead-Sea-pool-turns-BLOOD-RED-Bible-says-God-sent-angels-destroy-Sodom-Gomorrah.html

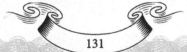

#47 - WHY IS RUSSIA BEGIN RESTORING THE ARC OF TRIUMPH IN SYRIA'S PALMYRA?

https://www.al-monitor.com/originals/2021/11/russia-begins-restoration-arc-triumph-syrias-palmyra

"16 The army had 200 million soldiers on horses. I heard them say how many there were. 17 I saw, as God wanted to show me, the horses and the men on them. The men had pieces of iron over their chests. These were red like fire and blue like the sky and yellow like sulphur. The heads of the horses looked like the heads of lions. Fire and smoke and sulphur came out of their mouths. 18 One-third part of all men was killed by the fire and smoke and sulphur that came out of their mouths."Revelation 9:16-18 https://www.biblegateway.com/passage/?search=Revelation%209%3A16-18&version=NLV

"And the name of the star is called Wormwood: and the third part of the waters became wormwood; and many men died of the waters, because they were made bitter."Revelation 8:11

#48 - DOES THE BIBLE TALK ABOUT THE RAPTURE & THE HARPAZO?

1st Thessalonians Chapter 4: 13-18 https://www.biblegateway.com/passage/?search=1%20Thessalonians%204&version=KJV

1st Thessalonians Chapter 4: 13-18 - "13 But I would not have you to be ignorant, brethren, concerning them which are asleep, that ye sorrow not, even as others which have <u>no hope.</u> 14 For if we believe that Jesus died and rose again, even so them also which sleep in Jesus will

Visit TimeToFreeAmerica.com/TheHomoDeuce to watch the video clips referenced throughout this book.

132

God bring with him. 15 For this we say unto you by the word of the Lord, that we which are alive and remain unto the coming of the Lord shall not prevent them which are asleep. 16 For the Lord himself shall descend from heaven with a shout, with the voice of the archangel, and with the trump of God: and the dead in Christ shall rise first: 17 Then we which are alive and remain shall be caught up together with them in the clouds, to meet the Lord in the air: and so shall we ever be with the Lord. 18 Wherefore comfort one another with these words."

....

Jesus was raptured

Enoch was raptured

Elijah was raptured

Caught up = Rapturo in Latin

Caught up = Harpazzo in Greek

Revelation 1:7 - Behold, he cometh with clouds; and every eye shall see him, and they also which pierced him: and all kindreds of the earth shall wail because of him. Even so, Amen.

....

1 Corinthians 15:52 - In a moment, in the twinkling of an eye, at the last trump: for the trumpet shall sound, and the dead shall be raised incorruptible, and we shall be changed.

....

#49 - EMMANUEL MACRON MEANING?

- Emmanuel = "God with us"   Macron is a mark

Visit TimeToFreeAmerica.com/TheHomoDeuce to watch the video clips referenced throughout this book.

Revelation 13: 16-18 - "16 And he causeth all, both small and great, rich and poor, free and bond, to receive a mark in their right hand, or in their foreheads: 17 And that no man might buy or sell, save he that had the mark, or the name of the beast, or the number of his name. 18 Here is wisdom. Let him that hath understanding count the number of the beast: for it is the number of a man; and his number is Six hundred threescore and six."Revelation 13: 16-18

#50 - WHY DOES EMMANUEL MACRON HANG OUT WITH YUVAL NOAH HARARI?

READ - https://www.thetimes.co.uk/imageserver/image/%2F-methode%2Ftimes%2Fprod%2Fweb%2Fbin%2Fa8414fa6-94b0-1 1e8-85e3-d844d3177259.jpg?crop=823%2C1234%2C50%2C250

#51 - ISRAEL 365 EXCLUSIVE: RED HEIFERS ARRIVE IN ISRAEL (WATCH):

READ: https://www.israel365news.com/274830/ watch-red-heifers-arrive-in-israel/

Numbers Chapter 19

"19 The Lord spoke to Moses and Aaron, saying, 2 "This is a statute of the law that the Lord has commanded: Tell the Israelites to bring you a red heifer without defect, in which there is no blemish and on

Visit TimeToFreeAmerica.com/TheHomoDeuce to watch
the video clips referenced throughout this book.

134

which no yoke has been laid. 3 You shall give it to the priest Eleazar, and it shall be taken outside the camp and slaughtered in his presence. 4 The priest Eleazar shall take some of its blood with his finger and sprinkle it seven times toward the front of the tent of meeting. 5 Then the heifer shall be burned in his sight; its skin, its flesh, and its blood, with its entrails,[a] shall be burned. 6 The priest shall take cedarwood, hyssop, and crimson material and throw them into the fire in which the heifer is burning. 7 Then the priest shall wash his clothes and bathe his body in water, and afterward he may come into the camp, but the priest shall remain unclean until evening. 8 The one who burns the heifer[b] shall wash his clothes in water and bathe his body in water; he shall remain unclean until evening. 9 Then someone who is clean shall gather up the ashes of the heifer and deposit them outside the camp in a clean place, and they shall be kept for the congregation of the Israelites for the water for cleansing. It is a purification offering. 10 The one who gathers the ashes of the heifer shall wash his clothes and be unclean until evening."

#52 - TRANSHUMANISM INVOLVES MERGING MAN AND MACHINE

"And whereas thou sawest iron mixed with miry clay, they shall mingle themselves with the seed of men: but they shall not cleave one to another, even as iron is not mixed with clay."Daniel 2:43

WATCH - Ray Kurzweil | Yuval Noah Harari Mentor and Director of Engineering at Google "We Are Going to Make Ourselves Smarter by Literally Merging with A.I."https:// rumble.com/v1prtwx-ray-kurzweil-yuval-noah-harari-mentor-and-director-of-engineering-at-google.html

Visit TimeToFreeAmerica.com/TheHomoDeuce to watch the video clips referenced throughout this book.

WATCH - *Ray Kurzweil | "We Will Connect Wirelessly Our Neocortex to the Cloud (with Nanobots That Enter Your Neocortex)."WATCH -* https://rumble.com/v1q5tq3-ray-kurzweil-we-will-connect-wirelessly-our-neocortex-to-the-cloud.html

WATCH - *Ray Kurzweil | "The Devices Will Be Inside Our Bodies and Brains. We Will Connect the Top Layer of Our Neocortex to Synthetic Neocortex In the Cloud." Ray Kurzweil - The Director of Engineering at Google and Yuval Noah Harari Mentor -* https://rumble.com/v1q1j9m-ray-kurzweil-the-devices-will-be-inside-our-bodies-and-brains,.html

WATCH - *Transhumanism | Joe Allen Explains Joe Biden's HORRIFYING Executive Order: Advancing Biotechnology and Biomanufacturing Innovation for a Sustainable, Safe, and Secure American Bioeconomy (READ the Executive Order In the Description) - WATCH -* https://rumble.com/v1kxiqf-transhumanism-joe-allen-explains-joe-bidens-horrifying-executive-order.html

#53 - IS "THE FOURTH INDUSTRIAL REVOLUTION" THE FULFILLMENT OF DANIEL'S PROPHECY OF A "FOURTH KINGDOM UPON THE EARTH?"

"Thus he said, The fourth beast shall be the fourth kingdom upon earth, which shall be diverse from all kingdoms, and shall devour the whole earth, and shall tread it down, and break it in pieces."Daniel 7:23

Visit TimeToFreeAmerica.com/TheHomoDeuce to watch the video clips referenced throughout this book.

WATCH - Joe Biden | Why Did Biden Deliver the Keynote In 2016 At the World Economic Forum On "Mastering the Fourth Industrial Revolution / The Great Reset?"https:// rumble.com/v1itvsx-joe-biden-why-did-biden.html

---

»Did Kim Clement See Emergence of the Fourth Reich and the Rise of the Nazi Party?

WATCH - https://www.youtube.com/watch?v=5nWr7koIOxo

»Why Does Klaus Schwab Refer to "The Great Reset" As "The Fourth Industrial Revolution?" Why Does Klaus Schwab Say That the "Fourth Industrial Revolution Will Change Not Only What We Do But Also Who We Are?"

WATCH - "Fourth Industrial Revolution Will Change Not Only What We Do But Also Who We Are."Klaus Schwab (Founder of the World Economic Forum)

https://rumble.com/v1c405t-klaus-schwab-fourth-industri- al-revolution-will-change-not-only-what-we-do-b.html

#54 - WHY IS THE MILITARY CALLING THEIR SWARM DRONE TECHNOLOGY "LOCUST?"

Revelation Chapter 9: "1 And the fifth angel sounded, and I saw a star fall from heaven unto the earth: and to him was given the key of the bottomless pit. 2 And he opened the bottomless pit; and there arose a smoke out of the pit, as the smoke of a great furnace;

Visit TimeToFreeAmerica.com/TheHomoDeuce to watch the video clips referenced throughout this book.

and the sun and the air were darkened by reason of the smoke of the pit. 3 And there came out of the smoke locusts upon the earth: and unto them was given power, as the scorpions of the earth have power. 4 And it was commanded them that they should not hurt the grass of the earth, neither any green thing, neither any tree; but only those men which have not the seal of God in their foreheads. 5 And to them it was given that they should not kill them, but that they should be tormented five months: and their torment was as the torment of a scorpion, when he striketh a man."

WATCH - Locust: https://m.youtube.com/watch?v=KLmmPnMvwNY

WATCH - Locust: https://www.businessinsider.com/china-launches-worlds-first-ai-unmanned-drone-aircraft-carrier-2022-6?amp

WATCH - LOCUST | Why Is the U.S. Army New Drone Swarm Drone Weapon Named "LOCUST"? - https://rumble.com/v1bv3x3-locust-why-u.s.-army-new-drone-swarm-drone-weapon-named-locust.html

» Why Is the NASA Crew Mascot An Extraterrestrial Locust?

https://mail.google.com/mail/u/0/#inbox/FM-fcgzGqQvzsvFBCFgQpPjwJXDFdFTlV

#55 - WILL A WAR BETWEEN RUSSIAN AND ISRAEL OCCUR BEFORE THE RAPTURE?

· *See the Chart: https://www.dropbox.com/s/e00ksx38x-u9ntvt/Ezekial%2038-39%20VS%20Revelation%20Description%20of%20Armageddon%20CHART.pdf?dl=0*

Visit TimeToFreeAmerica.com/TheHomoDeuce to watch the video clips referenced throughout this book.

READ - Ezekiel 38-39

"38 And the word of the Lord came unto me, saying, 2 Son of man, set thy face against Gog, the land of Magog, the chief prince of Meshech and Tubal, and prophesy against him, 3 And say, Thus saith the Lord God; Behold, I am against thee, O Gog, the chief prince of Meshech and Tubal: 4 And I will turn thee back, and put hooks into thy jaws, and I will bring thee forth, and all thine army, horses and horsemen, all of them clothed with all sorts of armour, even a great company with bucklers and shields, all of them handling swords: 5 Persia, Ethiopia, and Libya with them; all of them with shield and helmet: 6 Gomer, and all his bands; the house of Togarmah of the north quarters, and all his bands: and many people with thee. 7 Be thou prepared, and prepare for thyself, thou, and all thy company that are assembled unto thee, and be thou a guard unto them. 8 After many days thou shalt be visited: in the latter years thou shalt come into the land that is brought back from the sword, and is gathered out of many people, against the mountains of Israel, which have been always waste: but it is brought forth out of the nations, and they shall dwell safely all of them. 9 Thou shalt ascend and come like a storm, thou shalt be like a cloud to cover the land, thou, and all thy bands, and many people with thee. 10 Thus saith the Lord God; It shall also come to pass, that at the same time shall things come into thy mind, and thou shalt think an evil thought: 11 And thou shalt say, I will go up to the land of unwalled villages; I will go to them that are at rest, that dwell safely, all of them dwelling without walls, and having neither bars nor gates, 12 To take a spoil, and to take a prey; to turn thine hand upon the desolate places that are now inhabited, and upon the people that are gathered out of the nations, which have gotten cattle and goods, that dwell in the midst of the land. 13 Sheba, and Dedan, and the merchants of Tarshish, with all the young lions*

Visit TimeToFreeAmerica.com/TheHomoDeuce to watch
the video clips referenced throughout this book.

thereof, shall say unto thee, Art thou come to take a spoil? hast thou gathered thy company to take a prey? to carry away silver and gold, to take away cattle and goods, to take a great spoil? 14 Therefore, son of man, prophesy and say unto Gog, Thus saith the Lord God; In that day when my people of Israel dwelleth safely, shalt thou not know it? 15 And thou shalt come from thy place out of the north parts, thou, and many people with thee, all of them riding upon horses, a great company, and a mighty army: 16 And thou shalt come up against my people of Israel, as a cloud to cover the land; it shall be in the latter days, and I will bring thee against my land, that the heathen may know me, when I shall be sanctified in thee, O Gog, before their eyes. 17 Thus saith the Lord God; Art thou he of whom I have spoken in old time by my servants the prophets of Israel, which prophesied in those days many years that I would bring thee against them? 18 And it shall come to pass at the same time when Gog shall come against the land of Israel, saith the Lord God, that my fury shall come up in my face. 19 For in my jealousy and in the fire of my wrath have I spoken, Surely in that day there shall be a great shaking in the land of Israel; 20 So that the fishes of the sea, and the fowls of the heaven, and the beasts of the field, and all creeping things that creep upon the earth, and all the men that are upon the face of the earth, shall shake at my presence, and the mountains shall be thrown down, and the steep places shall fall, and every wall shall fall to the ground. 21 And I will call for a sword against him throughout all my mountains, saith the Lord God: every man's sword shall be against his brother. 22 And I will plead against him with pestilence and with blood; and I will rain upon him, and upon his bands, and upon the many people that are with him, an overflowing rain, and great hailstones, fire, and brimstone. 23 Thus will I magnify myself, and sanctify myself; and I will be known in the eyes of many nations, and they shall know that I am the Lord. 39 Therefore, thou son of man, prophesy against Gog, and say, Thus saith the Lord God; Behold, I am against thee, O Gog, the chief prince

Visit TimeToFreeAmerica.com/TheHomoDeuce to watch
the video clips referenced throughout this book.

of Meshech and Tubal: 2 And I will turn thee back, and leave but the sixth part of thee, and will cause thee to come up from the north parts, and will bring thee upon the mountains of Israel: 3 And I will smite thy bow out of thy left hand, and will cause thine arrows to fall out of thy right hand. 4 Thou shalt fall upon the mountains of Israel, thou, and all thy bands, and the people that is with thee: I will give thee unto the ravenous birds of every sort, and to the beasts of the field to be devoured. 5 Thou shalt fall upon the open field: for I have spoken it, saith the Lord God. 6 And I will send a fire on Magog, and among them that dwell carelessly in the isles: and they shall know that I am the Lord. 7 So will I make my holy name known in the midst of my people Israel; and I will not let them pollute my holy name any more: and the heathen shall know that I am the Lord, the Holy One in Israel. 8 Behold, it is come, and it is done, saith the Lord God; this is the day whereof I have spoken. 9 And they that dwell in the cities of Israel shall go forth, and shall set on fire and burn the weapons, both the shields and the bucklers, the bows and the arrows, and the hand-staves, and the spears, and they shall burn them with fire seven years: 10 So that they shall take no wood out of the field, neither cut down any out of the forests; for they shall burn the weapons with fire: and they shall spoil those that spoiled them, and rob those that robbed them, saith the Lord God. 11 And it shall come to pass in that day, that I will give unto Gog a place there of graves in Israel, the valley of the passengers on the east of the sea: and it shall stop the noses of the passengers: and there shall they bury Gog and all his multitude: and they shall call it The valley of Hamongog. 12 And seven months shall the house of Israel be burying of them, that they may cleanse the land. 13 Yea, all the people of the land shall bury them; and it shall be to them a renown the day that I shall be glorified, saith the Lord God. 14 And they shall sever out men of continual employment, passing through the land to bury with the passengers those that remain upon the face of the earth, to cleanse it: after the end of seven months shall

Visit TimeToFreeAmerica.com/TheHomoDeuce to watch
the video clips referenced throughout this book.

they search. 15 And the passengers that pass through the land, when any seeth a man's bone, then shall he set up a sign by it, till the buriers have buried it in the valley of Hamongog. 16 And also the name of the city shall be Hamonah. Thus shall they cleanse the land. 17 And, thou son of man, thus saith the Lord God; Speak unto every feathered fowl, and to every beast of the field, Assemble yourselves, and come; gather yourselves on every side to my sacrifice that I do sacrifice for you, even a great sacrifice upon the mountains of Israel, that ye may eat flesh, and drink blood. 18 Ye shall eat the flesh of the mighty, and drink the blood of the princes of the earth, of rams, of lambs, and of goats, of bullocks, all of them fatlings of Bashan. 19 And ye shall eat fat till ye be full, and drink blood till ye be drunken, of my sacrifice which I have sacrificed for you. 20 Thus ye shall be filled at my table with horses and chariots, with mighty men, and with all men of war, saith the Lord God. 21 And I will set my glory among the heathen, and all the heathen shall see my judgment that I have executed, and my hand that I have laid upon them. 22 So the house of Israel shall know that I am the Lord their God from that day and forward. 23 And the heathen shall know that the house of Israel went into captivity for their iniquity: because they trespassed against me, therefore hid I my face from them, and gave them into the hand of their enemies: so fell they all by the sword. 24 According to their uncleanness and accord-ing to their transgressions have I done unto them, and hid my face from them. 25 Therefore thus saith the Lord God; Now will I bring again the captivity of Jacob, and have mercy upon the whole house of Israel, and will be jealous for my holy name; 26 After that they have borne their shame, and all their trespasses whereby they have trespassed against me, when they dwelt safely in their land, and none made them afraid. 27 When I have brought them again from the people, and gathered them out of their enemies' lands, and am sanctified in them in the sight of many nations; 28 Then shall they know that I am the Lord their God, which caused them to be led into

Visit TimeToFreeAmerica.com/TheHomoDeuce to watch the video clips referenced throughout this book.

captivity among the heathen: but I have gathered them unto their own land, and have left none of them any more there. 29 Neither will I hide my face any more from them: for I have poured out my spirit upon the house of Israel, saith the Lord God."

#56 - WHY IS YUVAL NOAH HARARI TRYING TO INTRODUCE A NEW UNIVERSAL RELIGION WHILE ENCOURAGING PEOPLE TO TURN AWAY FROM GOD?

2nd Thessalonians Chapter 2:5-11 "Remember ye not, that, when I was yet with you, I told you these things? 6 And now ye know what withholdeth that he might be revealed in his time. 7 For the mystery of iniquity doth already work: only he who now letteth will let, until he be taken out of the way. 8 And then shall that Wicked be revealed, whom the Lord shall consume with the spirit of his mouth, and shall destroy with the brightness of his coming: 9 Even him, whose coming is after the working of Satan with all power and signs and lying wonders, 10 And with all deceivableness of unrighteousness in them that perish; because they received not the love of the truth, that they might be saved. 11 And for this cause God shall send them strong delusion, that they should believe a lie:"

WATCH - Yuval Noah Harari | The Anthropocene | What Is the Anthropocene? "You Learn As a Kid In the Book of Genesis That God Created Humans."<u>https://rumble.com/ v1onefz-yuval-noah-harari-the-anthropocene-.html</u>

WATCH - *Yuval Noah Harari | "Eternal Life"*

Visit TimeToFreeAmerica.com/TheHomoDeuce to watch the video clips referenced throughout this book.

Eternal Life."https://rumble.com/vymign-yuval-noah-harari-new-religions-will-offer-people-happiness-justice-and-ete.html

WATCH - Sergey Brin | Brainchips Eternal Life - https://rumble.com/v19e28v-sergey-brin-brainchips-eternal-life.html

WATCH - Elon Musk | We Could Merge with Artificial Intelligence Save State Eternal Life - https://rumble.com/v19e1e1-elon-musk-we-could-merge-with-artificial-intelligence-save-state-eternal-li.html

#57 - WHY IS YUVAL NOAH HARARI ATTEMPTING TO BAN THE EATING OF MEAT WHILE ENCOURAGING THE ENDING OF MARRIAGE AND CLEAR DEFINITION OF GENDERS?

2nd Thessalonians Chapter 2:12-15

"12 That they all might be damned who believed not the truth, but had pleasure in unrighteousness. 13 But we are bound to give thanks alway to God for you, brethren beloved of the Lord, because God hath from the beginning chosen you to salvation through sanctification of the Spirit and belief of the truth: 14 Whereunto he called you by our gospel, to the obtaining of the glory of our Lord Jesus Christ. 15 Therefore, brethren, stand fast, and hold the traditions which ye have been taught, whether by word, or our epistle."

Visit TimeToFreeAmerica.com/TheHomoDeuce to watch
the video clips referenced throughout this book.

144

WATCH - *Yuval Noah Harari | "The Clear Cut Dichotomy of Men and Women Will No Longer Make Any Sense."* *https://rumble.com/v1cakfr-yuval-noah-harari-the-clear-cut-dichotomy-of-men-and-women-will-no-longer-m.html*

WATCH - Yuval Noah Harari - *Yuval Noah Harari | Ending Marriage | "You Don't Need Children, You Can Have a Pension Fund. You Don't Need Neighbors, Sisters or Brothers. The State Provides You With Everything."* *https://rumble.com/v1ch7et-yuval-noah-harari-.html*

WATCH - *Yuval Noah Harari | Marriage | "People Having Relationships with Virtual Spouses. The Masses Don't Stand Much of a Chance."* *https://rumble.com/v1cm0s9-yuval-noah-harari-marriage-.html*

#58 - WHY ARE BILL GATES AND MIT ATTEMPTING TO DIM THE SUN?

"24 "But in those days, following that distress, " 'the sun will be darkened, and the moon will not give its light; 25 the stars will fall from the sky, and the heavenly bodies will be shaken.' 26 "At that time people will see the Son of Man coming in clouds with great power and glory. 27 And he will send his angels and gather his elect from the four winds, from the ends of the earth to the ends of the heavens."Mark 13:24-27

https://senseable.mit.edu/space-bubbles/

WATCH - *Climate Emergency | "World Economic Forum Pushes SPACE BUBBLES to Block Out the Sun and to Stop Climate Change"* *https://rumble.com/v1djf6n_climate-emergency-.html*

Visit TimeToFreeAmerica.com/TheHomoDeuce to watch the video clips referenced throughout this book.

#59- WHAT DOES THE BIBLE SAY ABOUT HYPER-INFLATION?

"And I heard a voice in the midst of the four beasts say, A measure of wheat for a penny, and three measures of barley for a penny; and see thou hurt not the oil and the wine."Revelation 6:6

WATCH - BRICS | As Saudi Arabia Joins BRICS Can BRICS De-Dollarize the Global Financial System? What Will Happen to the U.S. Dollar? - https://rumble.com/v1q8lbp-brics-as-saudi-arabia-joins-brics-can-brics.html

#60 - DO CHRISTIANS WIN IN THE END?

Revelation 20:2-5 - "2

He seized the dragon, that ancient serpent, who is the devil, or Satan, and bound him for a thousand years. 3 He threw him into the Abyss, and locked and sealed it over him, to keep him from deceiving the nations anymore until the thousand years were ended. After that, he must be set free for a short time. 4 I saw thrones on which were seated those who had been given authority to judge. And I saw the souls of those who had been beheaded because of their testimony about Jesus and because of the word of God. They had not worshiped the beast or its image and had not received its mark on their foreheads or their hands. They came to life and reigned with Christ for a thousand years. 5 (The rest of the dead did not come to life until the thousand years were ended.) This is the first resurrection."

Visit TimeToFreeAmerica.com/TheHomoDeuce to watch
the video clips referenced throughout this book.

146

1st Thessalonians Chapter 4: 13-18 -

"13 But I would not have you to be ignorant, brethren, concerning them which are asleep, that ye sorrow not, even as others which have <u>no hope.</u> 14 For if we believe that Jesus died and rose again, even so them also which sleep in Jesus will God bring with him. 15 For this we say unto you by the word of the Lord, that we which are alive and remain unto the coming of the Lord shall not prevent them which are asleep. 16 For the Lord himself shall descend from heaven with a shout, with the voice of the archangel, and with the trump of God: and the dead in Christ shall rise first: 17 Then we which are alive and remain shall be caught up together with them in the clouds, to meet the Lord in the air: and so shall we ever be with the Lord. 18 Wherefore comfort one another with these words."

Visit TimeToFreeAmerica.com/TheHomoDeuce to watch the video clips referenced throughout this book.

WORLD
ECONOMIC
FORUM

COVID-19:
THE GREAT
RESET

KLAUS SCHWAB
THIERRY MALLERET

THE GREAT
NARRATIVE
For a Better Future

KLAUS SCHWAB
THIERRY MALLERET

*Visit TimeToFreeAmerica.com/TheHomoDeuce to watch
the video clips referenced throughout this book.*

CHAPTER 6

So, What Can We Do Now?

The reason I started the ReAwaken America Tour and www.TimeToFreeAmerica.com is because I felt called by God to expose "The COVID-19 / Great Reset" agenda being pushed by Yuval Noah Harari, Klaus Schwab, Bill Gates, George Soros, China, and other elite globalists that hate God and America. The ReAwaken America Tour and this book exist to expose the election fraud, medical fraud, religious fraud, monetary fraud and mainstream media fraud that has been used to push the "COVID-19 Great Reset Agenda." Our call to action as Christians is to fulfill the great commission and to get people back to God because I believe that only true repentance and salvation can save this nation. – Clay Clark (The founder of The Thrivetime Show, and the organizer / emcee of The ReAwaken America Tour.

> »Mark 16:15 - **"And he said unto them, Go ye into all the world, and preach the gospel to every creature."**

> »Matthew 28:19 - "Go ye therefore, and teach all nations, baptizing them in the name of the Father, and of the Son, and of the Holy Ghost:"

Luke Chapter 9: 1-127

....

"1 Then he called his twelve disciples together, and gave them power and authority over all devils, and to cure diseases. 2 And he sent them to preach the kingdom of God, and to heal the sick. 3 And he said unto them, Take nothing for your journey, neither staves, nor scrip, neither bread, neither money; neither have two coats apiece. 4 And whatsoever house ye enter into, there abide, and thence depart. 5 And whosoever will not receive you, when ye go out of that city, shake off the very dust from your feet for a testimony against them. 6 And they departed, and went through the towns, preaching the gospel, and healing everywhere. 7 Now Herod the tetrarch heard of all that was done by him: and he was perplexed, because that it was said of some, that John was risen from the dead; 8 And of some, that Elias had appeared; and of others, that one of the old prophets was risen again. 9 And Herod said, John have I beheaded: but who is this, of whom I hear such things? And he desired to see him. 10 And the apostles, when they were returned, told him all that they had done. And he took them, and went aside privately into a desert place belonging to the city called Bethsaida. 11 And the people, when they knew it, followed him: and he received them, and spake unto them of the kingdom of God, and healed them that had need of healing. 12 And when the day began to wear away, then came the twelve, and said unto him, Send the multitude away, that they may go into the towns and country round about, and lodge, and get victuals: for we are here in a desert place. 13 But he said unto them, Give ye them to eat. And they said, We have no more but five loaves and two fishes; except we should go and buy meat for all this people. 14 For they were about five thousand men. And he said to his disciples, Make them sit down by fifties in a company. 15 And they did so, and made them all sit down. 16 Then he took the five loaves and the two fishes, and looking up to heaven, he blessed them, and brake, and gave to the disciples to set before

Visit TimeToFreeAmerica.com/TheHomoDeuce to watch the video clips referenced throughout this book.

the multitude. *17 And they did eat, and were all filled: and there was taken up of fragments that remained to them twelve baskets. 18 And it came to pass, as he was alone praying, his disciples were with him: and he asked them, saying, Whom say the people that I am? 19 They answering said, John the Baptist; but some say, Elias; and others say, that one of the old prophets is risen again. 20 He said unto them, But whom say ye that I am? Peter answering said, The Christ of God. 21 And he straitly charged them, and commanded them to tell no man that thing; 22 Saying, The Son of man must suffer many things, and be rejected of the elders and chief priests and scribes, and be slain, and be raised the third day. 23 And he said to them all, If any man will come after me, let him deny himself, and take up his cross daily, and follow me. 24 For whosoever will save his life shall lose it: but whosoever will lose his life for my sake, the same shall save it. 25 For what is a man advantaged, if he gain the whole world, and lose himself, or be cast away? 26 For whosoever shall be ashamed of me and of my words, of him shall the Son of man be ashamed, when he shall come in his own glory, and in his Father's, and of the holy angels. 27 But I tell you of a truth, there be some standing here, which shall not taste of death, till they see the kingdom of God."*

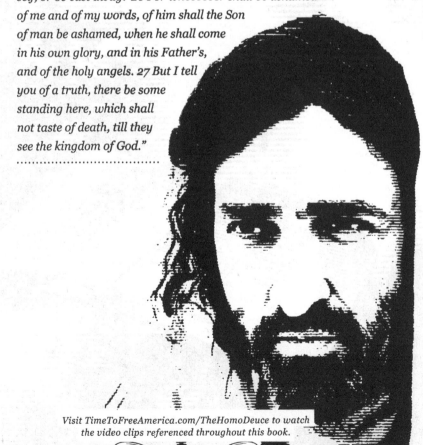

Visit *TimeToFreeAmerica.com/TheHomoDeuce* to watch
the video clips referenced throughout this book.

Visit TimeToFreeAmerica.com/TheHomoDeuce to watch
the video clips referenced throughout this book.

152

CHAPTER 7

What Does the Bible Have to Say About the Great Reset?

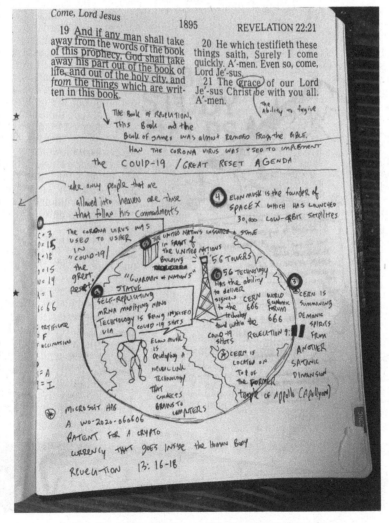

Visit TimeToFreeAmerica.com/TheHomoDeuce to watch the video clips referenced throughout this book.

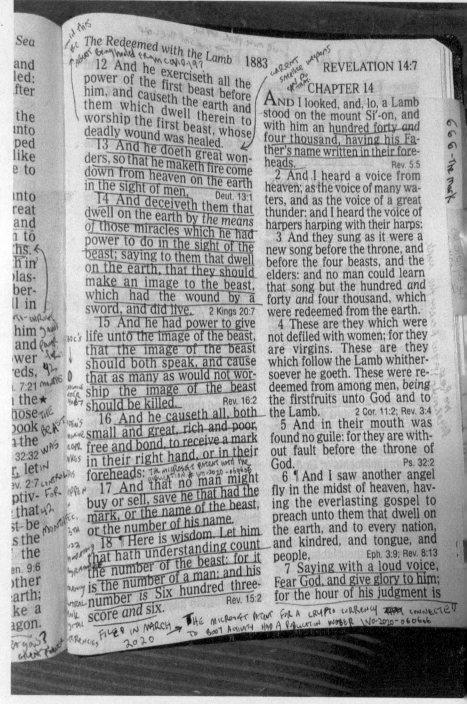

The Redeemed with the Lamb   1883

REVELATION 14:7

CHAPTER 14

12 And he exerciseth all the power of the first beast before him, and causeth the earth and them which dwell therein to worship the first beast, whose deadly wound was healed.

13 And he doeth great wonders, so that he maketh fire come down from heaven on the earth in the sight of men. *Deut. 13:1*

14 And deceiveth them that dwell on the earth by *the means* of those miracles which he had power to do in the sight of the beast; saying to them that dwell on the earth, that they should make an image to the beast, which had the wound by a sword, and did live. *2 Kings 20:7*

15 And he had power to give life unto the image of the beast, that the image of the beast should both speak, and cause that as many as would not worship the image of the beast should be killed. *Rev. 16:2*

16 And he causeth all, both small and great, rich and poor, free and bond, to receive a mark in their right hand, or in their foreheads:

17 And that no man might buy or sell, save he that had the mark, or the name of the beast, or the number of his name.

18 ¶ Here is wisdom. Let him that hath understanding count the number of the beast: for it is the number of a man; and his number *is* Six hundred three-score and six. *Rev. 15:2*

And I looked, and, lo, a Lamb stood on the mount Si'-on, and with him an hundred forty *and* four thousand, having his Father's name written in their foreheads. *Rev. 5:5*

2 And I heard a voice from heaven, as the voice of many waters, and as the voice of a great thunder: and I heard the voice of harpers harping with their harps:

3 And they sung as it were a new song before the throne, and before the four beasts, and the elders: and no man could learn that song but the hundred *and* forty *and* four thousand, which were redeemed from the earth.

4 These are they which were not defiled with women; for they are virgins. These are they which follow the Lamb whithersoever he goeth. These were redeemed from among men, *being* the firstfruits unto God and to the Lamb. *2 Cor. 11:2; Rev. 3:4*

5 And in their mouth was found no guile: for they are without fault before the throne of God. *Ps. 32:2*

6 ¶ And I saw another angel fly in the midst of heaven, having the everlasting gospel to preach unto them that dwell on the earth, and to every nation, and kindred, and tongue, and people, *Eph. 3:9; Rev. 8:13*

7 Saying with a loud voice, Fear God, and give glory to him; for the hour of his judgment is

Visit *TimeToFreeAmerica.com/TheHomoDeuce* to watch
the video clips referenced throughout this book.

154

...ylon Will Be Thrown Down **1889**

REVELATION 19:4

[handwritten:] HAS BIG PHARMA USED THEIR MONEY AND INFLUENCE TO PUT MRNA-MODIFYING SELF REPLICATING NANO-TECHNOLOGY

...nty and goodly are departed
...m thee, and thou shalt find
...m no more at all.
5 The merchants of these
...ngs, which were made rich by
..., shall stand afar off for the
...r of her torment, weeping and
...iling, *the world will not want to be associated* *[handwritten]*
...6 And saying, Alas, alas that
...eat city, that was clothed in *America* *[handwritten]*
...e linen, and purple, and scar-
... and decked with gold, and
...cious stones, and pearls!
...7 For in one hour so great
...hes is come to nought. And
...ery shipmaster, and all the
...mpany in ships, and sailors,
...d as many as trade by sea,
...od afar off,   Isa. 23:14
...18 And cried when they saw
...e smoke of her burning, say-
...g, What city is like unto this *is this referring to New York?* *[handwritten]*
...eat city!
...19 And they cast dust on their
...ads, and cried, weeping and
...iling, saying, Alas, alas that
...eat city, wherein were made
...h all that had ships in the sea
... reason of her costliness! for
... one hour is she made deso-
...te.   Josh. 7:6; Ezek. 27:30
...20 ¶ Rejoice over her, *thou*
...eaven, and ye holy apostles and
...ophets; for God hath avenged
...u on her.
...21 And a mighty angel took
... a stone like a great millstone,
...d cast *it* into the sea, saying,
...hus with violence shall that
...eat city Bab'-y-lon be thrown
...own, and shall be found no
...ore at all.   Jer. 51:64

[handwritten:] WILL A MONSOON OVERTAKE AN AMERICAN CITY?

22 And the voice of harpers, *inside of most people* *[handwritten]*
and musicians, and of pipers,
and trumpeters, shall be heard
no more at all in thee; and no
craftsman, of whatsoever craft
he be, shall be found any more
in thee; and the sound of a millstone shall be heard no more at
all in thee; *for the love of money is America* *[handwritten]*
23 And the light of a candle *the root of all evil* *[handwritten]*
shall shine no more at all in thee;
and the voice of the bridegroom
and of the bride shall be heard
no more at all in thee: for thy
merchants were the great men of
the earth; for by thy sorceries
were all nations deceived. *PHARMAKEON* *[handwritten]*
24 And in her was found the *pharm* *[handwritten]*
blood of prophets, and of saints,
and of all that were slain upon
the earth. *the WORLD ECONOMIC FORUM AND BIG PHARMA* *[handwritten]*

CHAPTER 19 *deceived the* *[handwritten]*

AND after these things I heard *entire world and* *[handwritten]*
a great voice of much people in
heaven, saying, Al-le-lu'-ia; Sal- *convinced* *[handwritten]*
vation, and glory, and honour, *them to* *[handwritten]*
and power, unto the Lord our
God: *is the great whore America?* *[handwritten]*
2 For true and righteous are *put* *[handwritten]*
his judgments: for he hath *RNA* *[handwritten]*
judged the great (whore) which *modifying* *[handwritten]*
did corrupt the earth with her *nano* *[handwritten]*
fornication, and hath avenged *tech* *[handwritten]*
the blood of his servants at her *inside* *[handwritten]*
hand.   Deut. 32:43 *their* *[handwritten]*
3 And again they said, Al-le- *bodies* *[handwritten]*
lu'-ia. And her smoke rose up for *that can* *[handwritten]*
ever and ever.   Isa. 34:10 *control* *[handwritten]*
4 And the four and twenty el- *their* *[handwritten]*
ders and the four beasts fell *thoughts* *[handwritten]*
down and worshipped God that

Visit TimeToFreeAmerica.com/TheHomoDeuce to watch
the video clips referenced throughout this book.

The Book of Daniel

THE PROPHET

Visit *TimeToFreeAmerica.com/TheHomoDeuce* to watch
the video clips referenced throughout this book.

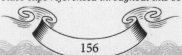

CHAPTER I

1 In the third year of the reign of Jehoiakim king of Judah came Nebuchadnezzar king of Babylon unto Jerusalem, and besieged it. 2 And the Lord gave Jehoiakim king of Judah into his hand, with part of the vessels of the house of God: which he carried into the land of Shinar to the house of his god; and he brought the vessels into the treasure house of his god. 3 And the king spake unto Ashpenaz the master of his eunuchs, that he should bring certain of the children of Israel, and of the king's seed, and of the princes; 4 Children in whom was no blemish, but well favoured, and skilful in all wisdom, and cunning in knowledge, and understanding science, and such as had ability in them to stand in the king's palace, and whom they might teach the learning and the tongue of the Chaldeans. 5 And the king appointed them a daily provision of the king's meat, and of the wine which he drank: so nourishing them three years, that at the end thereof they might stand before the king. 6 Now among these were of the children of Judah, Daniel, Hananiah, Mishael, and Azariah: 7 Unto whom the prince of the eunuchs gave names: for he gave unto Daniel the name of Belteshazzar; and to Hananiah, of Shadrach; and to Mishael, of Meshach; and to Azariah, of Abednego. 8 But Daniel purposed in his heart that he would

Visit TimeToFreeAmerica.com/TheHomoDeuce to watch the video clips referenced throughout this book.

not defile himself with the portion of the king's meat, nor with the wine which he drank: therefore he requested of the prince of the eunuchs that he might not defile himself. 9 Now God had brought Daniel into favour and tender love with the prince of the eunuchs. 10 And the prince of the eunuchs said unto Daniel, I fear my lord the king, who hath appointed your meat and your drink: for why should he see your faces worse liking than the children which are of your sort? then shall ye make me endanger my head to the king. 11 Then said Daniel to Melzar, whom the prince of the eunuchs had set over Daniel, Hananiah, Mishael, and Azariah, 12 Prove thy servants, I beseech thee, ten days; and let them give us pulse to eat, and water to drink. 13 Then let our countenances be looked upon before thee, and the countenance of the children that eat of the portion of the king's meat: and as thou seest, deal with thy servants. 14 So he consented to them in this matter, and proved them ten days. 15 And at the end of ten days their countenances appeared fairer and fatter in flesh than all the children which did eat the portion of the king's meat. 16 Thus Melzar took away the portion of their meat, and the wine that they should drink; and gave them pulse. 17 As for these four children, God gave them knowledge and skill in all learning and wisdom: and Daniel had understanding in all visions and dreams. 18 Now at the end of the days that the king had said he should bring them in, then the prince

Visit *TimeToFreeAmerica.com/TheHomoDeuce* to watch
the video clips referenced throughout this book.

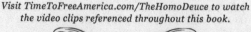

of the eunuchs brought them in before Nebuchadnezzar. 19 And the king communed with them; and among them all was found none like Daniel, Hananiah, Mishael, and Azariah: therefore stood they before the king. 20 And in all matters of wisdom and understanding, that the king inquired of them, he found them ten times better than all the magicians and astrologers that were in all his realm. 21 And Daniel continued even unto the first year of king Cyrus.

CHAPTER 2

2 Then the king commanded to call the magicians, and the astrologers, and the sorcerers, and the Chaldeans, for to shew the king his dreams. So they came and stood before the king. 3 And the king said unto them, I have dreamed a dream, and my spirit was troubled to know the dream. 4 Then spake the Chaldeans to the king in Syriack, O king, live for ever: tell thy servants the dream, and we will shew the interpretation. 5 The king answered and said to the Chaldeans, The thing is gone from me: if ye will not make known unto me the dream, with the interpretation thereof, ye shall be cut in pieces, and your houses shall be made a dunghill. 6 But if ye shew the dream, and the interpretation thereof, ye shall receive of me gifts and rewards and great

Visit *TimeToFreeAmerica.com/TheHomoDeuce* to watch
the video clips referenced throughout this book.

honour: therefore shew me the dream, and the interpretation thereof. 7 They answered again and said, Let the king tell his servants the dream, and we will shew the interpretation of it. 8 The king answered and said, I know of certainty that ye would gain the time, because ye see the thing is gone from me. 9 But if ye will not make known unto me the dream, there is but one decree for you: for ye have prepared lying and corrupt words to speak before me, till the time be changed: therefore tell me the dream, and I shall know that ye can shew me the interpretation thereof. 10 The Chaldeans answered before the king, and said, There is not a man upon the earth that can shew the king's matter: therefore there is no king, lord, nor ruler, that asked such things at any magician, or astrologer, or Chaldean. 11 And it is a rare thing that the king requireth, and there is none other that can shew it before the king, except the gods, whose dwelling is not with flesh. 12 For this cause the king was angry and very furious, and commanded to destroy all the wise men of Babylon. 13 And the decree went forth that the wise men should be slain; and they sought Daniel and his fellows to be slain. 14 Then Daniel answered with counsel and wisdom to Arioch the captain of the king's guard, which was gone forth to slay the wise men of Babylon: 15 He answered and said to Arioch the king's captain, Why is the decree so hasty from the king? Then Arioch made the thing

Visit TimeToFreeAmerica.com/TheHomoDeuce to watch
the video clips referenced throughout this book.

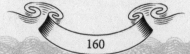

known to Daniel. 16 Then Daniel went in, and desired of the king that he would give him time, and that he would shew the king the interpretation. 17 Then Daniel went to his house, and made the thing known to Hananiah, Mishael, and Azariah, his companions: 18 That they would desire mercies of the God of heaven concerning this secret; that Daniel and his fellows should not perish with the rest of the wise men of Babylon. 19 Then was the secret revealed unto Daniel in a night vision. Then Daniel blessed the God of heaven. 20 Daniel answered and said, Blessed be the name of God for ever and ever: for wisdom and might are his: 21 And he changeth the times and the seasons: he removeth kings, and setteth up kings: he giveth wisdom unto the wise, and knowledge to them that know understanding: 22 He revealeth the deep and secret things: he knoweth what is in the darkness, and the light dwelleth with him. 23 I thank thee, and praise thee, O thou God of my fathers, who hast given me wisdom and might, and hast made known unto me now what we desired of thee: for thou hast now made known unto us the king's matter. 24 Therefore Daniel went in unto Arioch, whom the king had ordained to destroy the wise men of Babylon: he went and said thus unto him; Destroy not the wise men of Babylon: bring me in before the king, and I will shew unto the king the interpretation. 25 Then Arioch brought in Daniel before the king in haste, and said thus unto him, I

Visit TimeToFreeAmerica.com/TheHomoDeuce to watch the video clips referenced throughout this book.

have found a man of the captives of Judah, that will make known unto the king the interpretation. 26 The king answered and said to Daniel, whose name was Belteshazzar, Art thou able to make known unto me the dream which I have seen, and the interpretation thereof? 27 Daniel answered in the presence of the king, and said, The secret which the king hath demanded cannot the wise men, the astrologers, the magicians, the soothsayers, shew unto the king; 28 But there is a God in heaven that revealeth secrets, and maketh known to the king Nebuchadnezzar what shall be in the latter days. Thy dream, and the visions of thy head upon thy bed, are these; 29 As for thee, O king, thy thoughts came into thy mind upon thy bed, what should come to pass hereafter: and he that revealeth secrets maketh known to thee what shall come to pass. 30 But as for me, this secret is not revealed to me for any wisdom that I have more than any living, but for their sakes that shall make known the interpretation to the king, and that thou mightest know the thoughts of thy heart. 31 Thou, O king, sawest, and behold a great image. This great image, whose brightness was excellent, stood before thee; and the form thereof was terrible. 32 This image's head was of fine gold, his breast and his arms of silver, his belly and his thighs of brass, 33 His legs of iron, his feet part of iron and part of clay. 34 Thou sawest till that a stone was cut out without hands, which smote the image upon his feet that

Visit *TimeToFreeAmerica.com/TheHomoDeuce* to watch
the video clips referenced throughout this book.

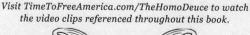

were of iron and clay, and brake them to pieces. 35 Then was the iron, the clay, the brass, the silver, and the gold, broken to pieces together, and became like the chaff of the summer threshingfloors; and the wind carried them away, that no place was found for them: and the stone that smote the image became a great mountain, and filled the whole earth. 36 This is the dream; and we will tell the interpretation thereof before the king. 37 Thou, O king, art a king of kings: for the God of heaven hath given thee a kingdom, power, and strength, and glory. 38 And wheresoever the children of men dwell, the beasts of the field and the fowls of the heaven hath he given into thine hand, and hath made thee ruler over them all. Thou art this head of gold. 39 And after thee shall arise another kingdom inferior to thee, and another third kingdom of brass, which shall bear rule over all the earth. 40 And the fourth kingdom shall be strong as iron: forasmuch as iron breaketh in pieces and subdueth all things: and as iron that breaketh all these, shall it break in pieces and bruise. 41 And whereas thou sawest the feet and toes, part of potters' clay, and part of iron, the kingdom shall be divided; but there shall be in it of the strength of the iron, forasmuch as thou sawest the iron mixed with miry clay. 42 And as the toes of the feet were part of iron, and part of clay, so the kingdom shall be partly strong, and partly broken. 43 And whereas thou sawest iron mixed with miry clay, they shall

Visit TimeToFreeAmerica.com/TheHomoDeuce to watch the video clips referenced throughout this book.

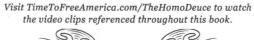

mingle themselves with the seed of men: but they shall not cleave one to another, even as iron is not mixed with clay. 44 And in the days of these kings shall the God of heaven set up a kingdom, which shall never be destroyed: and the kingdom shall not be left to other people, but it shall break in pieces and consume all these kingdoms, and it shall stand for ever. 45 Forasmuch as thou sawest that the stone was cut out of the mountain without hands, and that it brake in pieces the iron, the brass, the clay, the silver, and the gold; the great God hath made known to the king what shall come to pass hereafter: and the dream is certain, and the interpretation thereof sure. 46 Then the king Nebuchadnezzar fell upon his face, and worshipped Daniel, and commanded that they should offer an oblation and sweet odours unto him. 47 The king answered unto Daniel, and said, Of a truth it is, that your God is a God of gods, and a Lord of kings, and a revealer of secrets, seeing thou couldest reveal this secret. 48 Then the king made Daniel a great man, and gave him many great gifts, and made him ruler over the whole province of Babylon, and chief of the governors over all the wise men of Babylon. 49 Then Daniel requested of the king, and he set Shadrach, Meshach, and Abed-nego, over the affairs of the province of Babylon: but Daniel sat in the gate of the king.

Visit *TimeToFreeAmerica.com/TheHomoDeuce* to watch
the video clips referenced throughout this book.

CHAPTER 3

1 Nebuchadnezzar the king made an image of gold, whose height was threescore cubits, and the breadth thereof six cubits: he set it up in the plain of Dura, in the province of Babylon. 2 Then Nebuchadnezzar the king sent to gather together the princes, the governors, and the captains, the judges, the treasurers, the counsellers, the sheriffs, and all the rulers of the provinces, to come to the dedication of the image which Nebuchadnezzar the king had set up. 3 Then the princes, the governors, and captains, the judges, the treasurers, the counsellers, the sheriffs, and all the rulers of the provinces, were gathered together unto the dedication of the image that Nebuchadnezzar the king had set up; and they stood before the image that Nebuchadnezzar had set up. 4 Then an herald cried aloud, To you it is commanded, O people, nations, and languages, 5 That at what time ye hear the sound of the cornet, flute, harp, sackbut, psaltery, dulcimer, and all kinds of musick, ye fall down and worship the golden image that Nebuchadnezzar the king hath set up: 6 And whoso falleth not down and worshippeth shall the same hour be cast into the midst of a burning fiery furnace. 7 Therefore at that time, when all the people heard the sound of the cornet, flute, harp, sackbut, psaltery, and all kinds of musick, all the people, the nations, and the

Visit *TimeToFreeAmerica.com/TheHomoDeuce to watch the video clips referenced throughout this book.*

languages, fell down and worshipped the golden image that Nebuchadnezzar the king had set up. 8 Wherefore at that time certain Chaldeans came near, and accused the Jews. 9 They spake and said to the king Nebuchadnezzar, O king, live for ever. 10 Thou, O king, hast made a decree, that every man that shall hear the sound of the cornet, flute, harp, sackbut, psaltery, and dulcimer, and all kinds of musick, shall fall down and worship the golden image: 11 And whoso falleth not down and worshippeth, that he should be cast into the midst of a burning fiery furnace. 12 There are certain Jews whom thou hast set over the affairs of the province of Babylon, Shadrach, Meshach, and Abed-nego; these men, O king, have not regarded thee: they serve not thy gods, nor worship the golden image which thou hast set up. 13 Then Nebuchadnezzar in his rage and fury commanded to bring Shadrach, Meshach, and Abed-nego. Then they brought these men before the king. 14 Nebuchadnezzar spake and said unto them, Is it true, O Shadrach, Meshach, and Abed-nego, do not ye serve my gods, nor worship the golden image which I have set up? 15 Now if ye be ready that at what time ye hear the sound of the cornet, flute, harp, sackbut, psaltery, and dulcimer, and all kinds of musick, ye fall down and worship the image which I have made; well: but if ye worship not, ye shall be cast the same hour into the midst of a burning fiery furnace; and who is that God that shall deliver you out of my hands? 16

Visit TimeToFreeAmerica.com/TheHomoDeuce to watch the video clips referenced throughout this book.

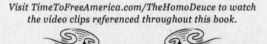

Shadrach, Meshach, and Abed-nego, answered and said to the king, O Nebuchadnezzar, we are not careful to answer thee in this matter. 17 If it be so, our God whom we serve is able to deliver us from the burning fiery furnace, and he will deliver us out of thine hand, O king. 18 But if not, be it known unto thee, O king, that we will not serve thy gods, nor worship the golden image which thou hast set up. 19 Then was Nebuchadnezzar full of fury, and the form of his visage was changed against Shadrach, Meshach, and Abed-nego: therefore he spake, and commanded that they should heat the furnace one seven times more than it was wont to be heated. 20 And he commanded the most mighty men that were in his army to bind Shadrach, Meshach, and Abed-nego, and to cast them into the burning fiery furnace. 21 Then these men were bound in their coats, their hosen, and their hats, and their other garments, and were cast into the midst of the burning fiery furnace. 22 Therefore because the king's commandment was urgent, and the furnace exceeding hot, the flame of the fire slew those men that took up Shadrach, Meshach, and Abed-nego. 23 And these three men, Shadrach, Meshach, and Abed-nego, fell down bound into the midst of the burning fiery furnace. 24 Then Nebuchadnezzar the king was astonied, and rose up in haste, and spake, and said unto his counsellers, Did not we cast three men bound into the midst of the fire? They answered and said unto the king, True, O king. 25 He

Visit *TimeToFreeAmerica.com/TheHomoDeuce* to watch
the video clips referenced throughout this book.

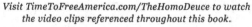

answered and said, Lo, I see four men loose, walking in the midst of the fire, and they have no hurt; and the form of the fourth is like the Son of God. 26 Then Nebuchadnezzar came near to the mouth of the burning fiery furnace, and spake, and said, Shadrach, Meshach, and Abed-nego, ye servants of the most high God, come forth, and come hither. Then Shadrach, Meshach, and Abed-nego, came forth of the midst of the fire. 27 And the princes, governors, and captains, and the king's counsellers, being gathered together, saw these men, upon whose bodies the fire had no power, nor was an hair of their head singed, neither were their coats changed, nor the smell of fire had passed on them. 28 Then Nebuchadnezzar spake, and said, Blessed be the God of Shadrach, Meshach, and Abed-nego, who hath sent his angel, and delivered his servants that trusted in him, and have changed the king's word, and yielded their bodies, that they might not serve nor worship any god, except their own God. 29 Therefore I make a decree, That every people, nation, and language, which speak any thing amiss against the God of Shadrach, Meshach, and Abed-nego, shall be cut in pieces, and their houses shall be made a dunghill: because there is no other God that can deliver after this sort. 30 Then the king promoted Shadrach, Meshach, and Abed-nego, in the province of Babylon.

Visit *TimeToFreeAmerica.com/TheHomoDeuce* to watch the video clips referenced throughout this book.

CHAPTER 4

1 Nebuchadnezzar the king, unto all people, nations, and languages, that dwell in all the earth; Peace be multiplied unto you. 2 I thought it good to shew the signs and wonders that the high God hath wrought toward me. 3 How great are his signs! and how mighty are his wonders! his kingdom is an everlasting kingdom, and his dominion is from generation to generation. 4 I Nebuchadnezzar was at rest in mine house, and flourishing in my palace: 5 I saw a dream which made me afraid, and the thoughts upon my bed and the visions of my head troubled me. 6 Therefore made I a decree to bring in all the wise men of Babylon before me, that they might make known unto me the interpretation of the dream. 7 Then came in the magicians, the astrologers, the Chaldeans, and the soothsayers: and I told the dream before them; but they did not make known unto me the interpretation thereof. 8 But at the last Daniel came in before me, whose name was Belteshazzar, according to the name of my god, and in whom is the spirit of the holy gods: and before him I told the dream, saying, 9 O Belteshazzar, master of the magicians, because I know that the spirit of the holy gods is in thee, and no secret troubleth thee, tell me the visions of my dream that I have seen, and the interpretation thereof. 10 Thus were the

Visit TimeToFreeAmerica.com/TheHomoDeuce to watch the video clips referenced throughout this book.

visions of mine head in my bed; I saw, and behold a tree in the midst of the earth, and the height thereof was great. 11 The tree grew, and was strong, and the height thereof reached unto heaven, and the sight thereof to the end of all the earth: 12 The leaves thereof were fair, and the fruit thereof much, and in it was meat for all: the beasts of the field had shadow under it, and the fowls of the heaven dwelt in the boughs thereof, and all flesh was fed of it. 13 I saw in the visions of my head upon my bed, and, behold, a watcher and an holy one came down from heaven; 14 He cried aloud, and said thus, Hew down the tree, and cut off his branches, shake off his leaves, and scatter his fruit: let the beasts get away from under it, and the fowls from his branches: 15 Nevertheless leave the stump of his roots in the earth, even with a band of iron and brass, in the tender grass of the field; and let it be wet with the dew of heaven, and let his portion be with the beasts in the grass of the earth: 16 Let his heart be changed from man's, and let a beast's heart be given unto him; and let seven times pass over him. 17 This matter is by the decree of the watchers, and the demand by the word of the holy ones: to the intent that the living may know that the most High ruleth in the kingdom of men, and giveth it to whomsoever he will, and setteth up over it the basest of men. 18 This dream I king Nebuchadnezzar have seen. Now thou, O Belteshazzar, declare the interpretation thereof, forasmuch as all the

Visit *TimeToFreeAmerica.com/TheHomoDeuce* to watch
the video clips referenced throughout this book.

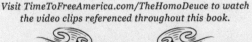

wise men of my kingdom are not able to make known unto me the interpretation: but thou art able; for the spirit of the holy gods is in thee. 19 Then Daniel, whose name was Belteshazzar, was astonied for one hour, and his thoughts troubled him. The king spake, and said, Belteshazzar, let not the dream, or the interpretation thereof, trouble thee. Belteshazzar answered and said, My lord, the dream be to them that hate thee, and the interpretation thereof to thine enemies. 20 The tree that thou sawest, which grew, and was strong, whose height reached unto the heaven, and the sight thereof to all the earth; 21 Whose leaves were fair, and the fruit thereof much, and in it was meat for all; under which the beasts of the field dwelt, and upon whose branches the fowls of the heaven had their habitation: 22 It is thou, O king, that art grown and become strong: for thy greatness is grown, and reacheth unto heaven, and thy dominion to the end of the earth. 23 And whereas the king saw a watcher and an holy one coming down from heaven, and saying, Hew the tree down, and destroy it; yet leave the stump of the roots thereof in the earth, even with a band of iron and brass, in the tender grass of the field; and let it be wet with the dew of heaven, and let his portion be with the beasts of the field, till seven times pass over him; 24 This is the interpretation, O king, and this is the decree of the most High, which is come upon my lord the king: 25 That they shall drive thee from men, and thy dwelling

Visit *TimeToFreeAmerica.com/TheHomoDeuce* to watch
the video clips referenced throughout this book.

shall be with the beasts of the field, and they shall make thee to eat grass as oxen, and they shall wet thee with the dew of heaven, and seven times shall pass over thee, till thou know that the most High ruleth in the kingdom of men, and giveth it to whomsoever he will. 26 And whereas they commanded to leave the stump of the tree roots; thy kingdom shall be sure unto thee, after that thou shalt have known that the heavens do rule. 27 Wherefore, O king, let my counsel be acceptable unto thee, and break off thy sins by righteousness, and thine iniquities by shewing mercy to the poor; if it may be a lengthening of thy tranquillity. 28 All this came upon the king Nebuchadnezzar. 29 At the end of twelve months he walked in the palace of the kingdom of Babylon. 30 The king spake, and said, Is not this great Babylon, that I have built for the house of the kingdom by the might of my power, and for the honour of my majesty? 31 While the word was in the king's mouth, there fell a voice from heaven, saying, O king Nebuchadnezzar, to thee it is spoken; The kingdom is departed from thee. 32 And they shall drive thee from men, and thy dwelling shall be with the beasts of the field: they shall make thee to eat grass as oxen, and seven times shall pass over thee, until thou know that the most High ruleth in the kingdom of men, and giveth it to whomsoever he will. 33 The same hour was the thing fulfilled upon Nebuchadnezzar: and he was driven from men, and did eat grass as oxen, and his

Visit *TimeToFreeAmerica.com/TheHomoDeuce* to watch the video clips referenced throughout this book.

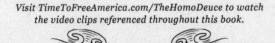

body was wet with the dew of heaven, till his hairs were grown like eagles' feathers, and his nails like birds' claws. 34 And at the end of the days I Nebuchadnezzar lifted up mine eyes unto heaven, and mine understanding returned unto me, and I blessed the most High, and I praised and honoured him that liveth for ever, whose dominion is an everlasting dominion, and his kingdom is from generation to generation: 35 And all the inhabitants of the earth are reputed as nothing: and he doeth according to his will in the army of heaven, and among the inhabitants of the earth: and none can stay his hand, or say unto him, What doest thou? 36 At the same time my reason returned unto me; and for the glory of my kingdom, mine honour and brightness returned unto me; and my counsellers and my lords sought unto me; and I was established in my kingdom, and excellent majesty was added unto me. 37 Now I Nebuchadnezzar praise and extol and honour the King of heaven, all whose works are truth, and his ways judgment: and those that walk in pride he is able to abase.

CHAPTER 5

1 Belshazzar the king made a great feast to a thousand of his lords, and drank wine before the thousand. 2 Belshazzar, whiles he tasted the wine, commanded to

Visit *TimeToFreeAmerica.com/TheHomoDeuce* to watch
the video clips referenced throughout this book.

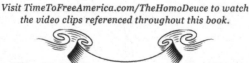

bring the golden and silver vessels which his father Nebuchadnezzar had taken out of the temple which was in Jerusalem; that the king, and his princes, his wives, and his concubines, might drink therein. 3 Then they brought the golden vessels that were taken out of the temple of the house of God which was at Jerusalem; and the king, and his princes, his wives, and his concubines, drank in them. 4 They drank wine, and praised the gods of gold, and of silver, of brass, of iron, of wood, and of stone. 5 In the same hour came forth fingers of a man's hand, and wrote over against the candlestick upon the plaister of the wall of the king's palace: and the king saw the part of the hand that wrote. 6 Then the king's countenance was changed, and his thoughts troubled him, so that the joints of his loins were loosed, and his knees smote one against another. 7 The king cried aloud to bring in the astrologers, the Chaldeans, and the soothsayers. And the king spake, and said to the wise men of Babylon, Whosoever shall read this writing, and shew me the interpretation thereof, shall be clothed with scarlet, and have a chain of gold about his neck, and shall be the third ruler in the kingdom. 8 Then came in all the king's wise men: but they could not read the writing, nor make known to the king the interpretation thereof. 9 Then was king Belshazzar greatly troubled, and his countenance was changed in him, and his lords were astonied. 10 Now the queen, by reason of the words

Visit TimeToFreeAmerica.com/TheHomoDeuce to watch the video clips referenced throughout this book.

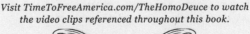

of the king and his lords, came into the banquet house: and the queen spake and said, O king, live for ever: let not thy thoughts trouble thee, nor let thy countenance be changed: 11 There is a man in thy kingdom, in whom is the spirit of the holy gods; and in the days of thy father light and understanding and wisdom, like the wisdom of the gods, was found in him; whom the king Nebuchadnezzar thy father, the king, I say, thy father, made master of the magicians, astrologers, Chaldeans, and soothsayers; 12 Forasmuch as an excellent spirit, and knowledge, and understanding, interpreting of dreams, and shewing of hard sentences, and dissolving of doubts, were found in the same Daniel, whom the king named Belteshazzar: now let Daniel be called, and he will shew the interpretation. 13 Then was Daniel brought in before the king. And the king spake and said unto Daniel, Art thou that Daniel, which art of the children of the captivity of Judah, whom the king my father brought out of Jewry? 14 I have even heard of thee, that the spirit of the gods is in thee, and that light and understanding and excellent wisdom is found in thee. 15 And now the wise men, the astrologers, have been brought in before me, that they should read this writing, and make known unto me the interpretation thereof: but they could not shew the interpretation of the thing: 16 And I have heard of thee, that thou canst make interpretations, and dissolve doubts: now if thou canst read the writing, and

Visit TimeToFreeAmerica.com/TheHomoDeuce to watch the video clips referenced throughout this book.

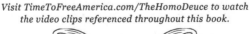

make known to me the interpretation thereof, thou shalt be clothed with scarlet, and have a chain of gold about thy neck, and shalt be the third ruler in the kingdom. 17 Then Daniel answered and said before the king, Let thy gifts be to thyself, and give thy rewards to another; yet I will read the writing unto the king, and make known to him the interpretation. 18 O thou king, the most high God gave Nebuchadnezzar thy father a kingdom, and majesty, and glory, and honour: 19 And for the majesty that he gave him, all people, nations, and languages, trembled and feared before him: whom he would he slew; and whom he would he kept alive; and whom he would he set up; and whom he would he put down. 20 But when his heart was lifted up, and his mind hardened in pride, he was deposed from his kingly throne, and they took his glory from him: 21 And he was driven from the sons of men; and his heart was made like the beasts, and his dwelling was with the wild asses: they fed him with grass like oxen, and his body was wet with the dew of heaven; till he knew that the most high God ruled in the kingdom of men, and that he appointeth over it whomsoever he will. 22 And thou his son, O Belshazzar, hast not humbled thine heart, though thou knewest all this; 23 But hast lifted up thyself against the Lord of heaven; and they have brought the vessels of his house before thee, and thou, and thy lords, thy wives, and thy concubines, have drunk wine in them; and thou hast praised the gods

Visit *TimeToFreeAmerica.com/TheHomoDeuce* to watch the video clips referenced throughout this book.

of silver, and gold, of brass, iron, wood, and stone, which see not, nor hear, nor know: and the God in whose hand thy breath is, and whose are all thy ways, hast thou not glorified: 24 Then was the part of the hand sent from him; and this writing was written. 25 And this is the writing that was written, MENE, MENE, TEKEL, UPHARSIN. 26 This is the interpretation of the thing: MENE; God hath numbered thy kingdom, and finished it. 27 TEKEL; Thou art weighed in the balances, and art found wanting. 28 PERES; Thy kingdom is divided, and given to the Medes and Persians. 29 Then commanded Belshazzar, and they clothed Daniel with scarlet, and put a chain of gold about his neck, and made a proclamation concerning him, that he should be the third ruler in the kingdom. 30 In that night was Belshazzar the king of the Chaldeans slain. 31 And Darius the Median took the kingdom, being about threescore and two years old.

CHAPTER 6

1 It pleased Darius to set over the kingdom an hundred and twenty princes, which should be over the whole kingdom; 2 And over these three presidents; of whom Daniel was first: that the princes might give accounts unto them, and the king should have no damage. 3 Then this

Visit TimeToFreeAmerica.com/TheHomoDeuce to watch
the video clips referenced throughout this book.

177

Daniel was preferred above the presidents and princes, because an excellent spirit was in him; and the king thought to set him over the whole realm. 4 Then the presidents and princes sought to find occasion against Daniel concerning the kingdom; but they could find none occasion nor fault; forasmuch as he was faithful, neither was there any error or fault found in him. 5 Then said these men, We shall not find any occasion against this Daniel, except we find it against him concerning the law of his God. 6 Then these presidents and princes assembled together to the king, and said thus unto him, King Darius, live for ever. 7 All the presidents of the kingdom, the governors, and the princes, the counsellers, and the captains, have consulted together to establish a royal statute, and to make a firm decree, that whosoever shall ask a petition of any God or man for thirty days, save of thee, O king, he shall be cast into the den of lions. 8 Now, O king, establish the decree, and sign the writing, that it be not changed, according to the law of the Medes and Persians, which altereth not. 9 Wherefore king Darius signed the writing and the decree. 10 Now when Daniel knew that the writing was signed, he went into his house; and his windows being open in his chamber toward Jerusalem, he kneeled upon his knees three times a day, and prayed, and gave thanks before his God, as he did aforetime. 11 Then these men assembled, and found Daniel praying and making supplication before his God. 12 Then

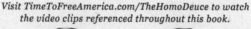

Visit *TimeToFreeAmerica.com/TheHomoDeuce* to watch the video clips referenced throughout this book.

they came near, and spake before the king concerning the king's decree; Hast thou not signed a decree, that every man that shall ask a petition of any God or man within thirty days, save of thee, O king, shall be cast into the den of lions? The king answered and said, The thing is true, according to the law of the Medes and Persians, which altereth not. 13 Then answered they and said before the king, That Daniel, which is of the children of the captivity of Judah, regardeth not thee, O king, nor the decree that thou hast signed, but maketh his petition three times a day. 14 Then the king, when he heard these words, was sore displeased with himself, and set his heart on Daniel to deliver him: and he laboured till the going down of the sun to deliver him. 15 Then these men assembled unto the king, and said unto the king, Know, O king, that the law of the Medes and Persians is, That no decree nor statute which the king establisheth may be changed. 16 Then the king commanded, and they brought Daniel, and cast him into the den of lions. Now the king spake and said unto Daniel, Thy God whom thou servest continually, he will deliver thee. 17 And a stone was brought, and laid upon the mouth of the den; and the king sealed it with his own signet, and with the signet of his lords; that the purpose might not be changed concerning Daniel. 18 Then the king went to his palace, and passed the night fasting: neither were instruments of musick brought before him: and his

Visit *TimeToFreeAmerica.com/TheHomoDeuce* to watch
the video clips referenced throughout this book.

sleep went from him. 19 Then the king arose very early in the morning, and went in haste unto the den of lions. 20 And when he came to the den, he cried with a lamentable voice unto Daniel: and the king spake and said to Daniel, O Daniel, servant of the living God, is thy God, whom thou servest continually, able to deliver thee from the lions? 21 Then said Daniel unto the king, O king, live for ever. 22 My God hath sent his angel, and hath shut the lions' mouths, that they have not hurt me: forasmuch as before him innocency was found in me; and also before thee, O king, have I done no hurt. 23 Then was the king exceeding glad for him, and commanded that they should take Daniel up out of the den. So Daniel was taken up out of the den, and no manner of hurt was found upon him, because he believed in his God. 24 And the king commanded, and they brought those men which had accused Daniel, and they cast them into the den of lions, them, their children, and their wives; and the lions had the mastery of them, and brake all their bones in pieces or ever they came at the bottom of the den. 25 Then king Darius wrote unto all people, nations, and languages, that dwell in all the earth; Peace be multiplied unto you. 26 I make a decree, That in every dominion of my kingdom men tremble and fear before the God of Daniel: for he is the living God, and stedfast for ever, and his kingdom that which shall not be destroyed, and his dominion shall be even unto the end.

Visit TimeToFreeAmerica.com/TheHomoDeuce to watch
the video clips referenced throughout this book.

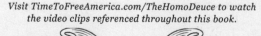

27 He delivereth and rescueth, and he worketh signs and wonders in heaven and in earth, who hath delivered Daniel from the power of the lions. 28 So this Daniel prospered in the reign of Darius, and in the reign of Cyrus the Persian.

CHAPTER 7

1 In the first year of Belshazzar king of Babylon Daniel had a dream and visions of his head upon his bed: then he wrote the dream, and told the sum of the matters. 2 Daniel spake and said, I saw in my vision by night, and, behold, the four winds of the heaven strove upon the great sea. 3 And four great beasts came up from the sea, diverse one from another. 4 The first was like a lion, and had eagle's wings: I beheld till the wings thereof were plucked, and it was lifted up from the earth, and made stand upon the feet as a man, and a man's heart was given to it. 5 And behold another beast, a second, like to a bear, and it raised up itself on one side, and it had three ribs in the mouth of it between the teeth of it: and they said thus unto it, Arise, devour much flesh. 6 After this I beheld, and lo another, like a leopard, which had upon the back of it four wings of a fowl; the beast had also four heads; and dominion was given to it. 7 After this I saw in the night visions, and behold a fourth beast, dreadful and terrible, and strong

Visit *TimeToFreeAmerica.com/TheHomoDeuce* to watch the video clips referenced throughout this book.

exceedingly; and it had great iron teeth: it devoured and brake in pieces, and stamped the residue with the feet of it: and it was diverse from all the beasts that were before it; and it had ten horns. 8 I considered the horns, and, behold, there came up among them another little horn, before whom there were three of the first horns plucked up by the roots: and, behold, in this horn were eyes like the eyes of man, and a mouth speaking great things. 9 I beheld till the thrones were cast down, and the Ancient of days did sit, whose garment was white as snow, and the hair of his head like the pure wool: his throne was like the fiery flame, and his wheels as burning fire. 10 A fiery stream issued and came forth from before him: thousand thousands ministered unto him, and ten thousand times ten thousand stood before him: the judgment was set, and the books were opened. 11 I beheld then because of the voice of the great words which the horn spake: I beheld even till the beast was slain, and his body destroyed, and given to the burning flame. 12 As concerning the rest of the beasts, they had their dominion taken away: yet their lives were prolonged for a season and time. 13 I saw in the night visions, and, behold, one like the Son of man came with the clouds of heaven, and came to the Ancient of days, and they brought him near before him. 14 And there was given him dominion, and glory, and a kingdom, that all people, nations, and languages, should serve him: his dominion is

Visit TimeToFreeAmerica.com/TheHomoDeuce to watch the video clips referenced throughout this book.

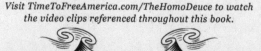

182

an everlasting dominion, which shall not pass away, and his kingdom that which shall not be destroyed. 15 I Daniel was grieved in my spirit in the midst of my body, and the visions of my head troubled me. 16 I came near unto one of them that stood by, and asked him the truth of all this. So he told me, and made me know the interpretation of the things. 17 These great beasts, which are four, are four kings, which shall arise out of the earth. 18 But the saints of the most High shall take the kingdom, and possess the kingdom for ever, even for ever and ever. 19 Then I would know the truth of the fourth beast, which was diverse from all the others, exceeding dreadful, whose teeth were of iron, and his nails of brass; which devoured, brake in pieces, and stamped the residue with his feet; 20 And of the ten horns that were in his head, and of the other which came up, and before whom three fell; even of that horn that had eyes, and a mouth that spake very great things, whose look was more stout than his fellows. 21 I beheld, and the same horn made war with the saints, and prevailed against them; 22 Until the Ancient of days came, and judgment was given to the saints of the most High; and the time came that the saints possessed the kingdom. 23 Thus he said, The fourth beast shall be the fourth kingdom upon earth, which shall be diverse from all kingdoms, and shall devour the whole earth, and shall tread it down, and break it in pieces. 24 And the ten horns out of this kingdom are ten kings that

Visit *TimeToFreeAmerica.com/TheHomoDeuce* to watch
the video clips referenced throughout this book.

shall arise: and another shall rise after them; and he shall be diverse from the first, and he shall subdue three kings. 25 And he shall speak great words against the most High, and shall wear out the saints of the most High, and think to change times and laws: and they shall be given into his hand until a time and times and the dividing of time. 26 But the judgment shall sit, and they shall take away his dominion, to consume and to destroy it unto the end. 27 And the kingdom and dominion, and the greatness of the kingdom under the whole heaven, shall be given to the people of the saints of the most High, whose kingdom is an everlasting kingdom, and all dominions shall serve and obey him. 28 Hitherto is the end of the matter. As for me Daniel, my cogitations much troubled me, and my countenance changed in me: but I kept the matter in my heart.

CHAPTER 8

1 In the third year of the reign of king Belshazzar a vision appeared unto me, even unto me Daniel, after that which appeared unto me at the first. 2 And I saw in a vision; and it came to pass, when I saw, that I was at Shushan in the palace, which is in the province of Elam; and I saw in a vision, and I was by the river of Ulai. 3 Then I lifted up

Visit TimeToFreeAmerica.com/TheHomoDeuce to watch the video clips referenced throughout this book.

mine eyes, and saw, and, behold, there stood before the river a ram which had two horns: and the two horns were high; but one was higher than the other, and the higher came up last. 4 I saw the ram pushing westward, and northward, and southward; so that no beasts might stand before him, neither was there any that could deliver out of his hand; but he did according to his will, and became great. 5 And as I was considering, behold, an he goat came from the west on the face of the whole earth, and touched not the ground: and the goat had a notable horn between his eyes. 6 And he came to the ram that had two horns, which I had seen standing before the river, and ran unto him in the fury of his power. 7 And I saw him come close unto the ram, and he was moved with choler against him, and smote the ram, and brake his two horns: and there was no power in the ram to stand before him, but he cast him down to the ground, and stamped upon him: and there was none that could deliver the ram out of his hand. 8 Therefore the he goat waxed very great: and when he was strong, the great horn was broken; and for it came up four notable ones toward the four winds of heaven. 9 And out of one of them came forth a little horn, which waxed exceeding great, toward the south, and toward the east, and toward the pleasant land. 10 And it waxed great, even to the host of heaven; and it cast down some of the host and of the stars to the ground, and stamped upon them. 11 Yea,

Visit *TimeToFreeAmerica.com/TheHomoDeuce* to watch
the video clips referenced throughout this book.

he magnified himself even to the prince of the host, and by him the daily sacrifice was taken away, and the place of his sanctuary was cast down. 12 And an host was given him against the daily sacrifice by reason of transgression, and it cast down the truth to the ground; and it practised, and prospered. 13 Then I heard one saint speaking, and another saint said unto that certain saint which spake, How long shall be the vision concerning the daily sacrifice, and the transgression of desolation, to give both the sanctuary and the host to be trodden under foot? 14 And he said unto me, Unto two thousand and three hundred days; then shall the sanctuary be cleansed. 15 And it came to pass, when I, even I Daniel, had seen the vision, and sought for the meaning, then, behold, there stood before me as the appearance of a man. 16 And I heard a man's voice between the banks of Ulai, which called, and said, Gabriel, make this man to understand the vision. 17 So he came near where I stood: and when he came, I was afraid, and fell upon my face: but he said unto me, Understand, O son of man: for at the time of the end shall be the vision. 18 Now as he was speaking with me, I was in a deep sleep on my face toward the ground: but he touched me, and set me upright. 19 And he said, Behold, I will make thee know what shall be in the last end of the indignation: for at the time appointed the end shall be. 20 The ram which thou sawest having two horns are the kings of Media and

Visit *TimeToFreeAmerica.com/TheHomoDeuce* to watch the video clips referenced throughout this book.

Persia. 21 And the rough goat is the king of Grecia: and the great horn that is between his eyes is the first king. 22 Now that being broken, whereas four stood up for it, four kingdoms shall stand up out of the nation, but not in his power. 23 And in the latter time of their kingdom, when the transgressors are come to the full, a king of fierce countenance, and understanding dark sentences, shall stand up. 24 And his power shall be mighty, but not by his own power: and he shall destroy wonderfully, and shall prosper, and practise, and shall destroy the mighty and the holy people. 25 And through his policy also he shall cause craft to prosper in his hand; and he shall magnify himself in his heart, and by peace shall destroy many: he shall also stand up against the Prince of princes; but he shall be broken without hand. 26 And the vision of the evening and the morning which was told is true: wherefore shut thou up the vision; for it shall be for many days. 27 And I Daniel fainted, and was sick certain days; afterward I rose up, and did the king's business; and I was astonished at the vision, but none understood it.

Visit *TimeToFreeAmerica.com/TheHomoDeuce to watch the video clips referenced throughout this book.*

CHAPTER 9

1 In the first year of Darius the son of Ahasuerus, of the seed of the Medes, which was made king over the realm of the Chaldeans; 2 In the first year of his reign I Daniel understood by books the number of the years, whereof the word of the LORD came to Jeremiah the prophet, that he would accomplish seventy years in the desolations of Jerusalem. 3 And I set my face unto the Lord God, to seek by prayer and supplications, with fasting, and sackcloth, and ashes: 4 And I prayed unto the LORD my God, and made my confession, and said, O Lord, the great and dreadful God, keeping the covenant and mercy to them that love him, and to them that keep his commandments; 5 We have sinned, and have committed iniquity, and have done wickedly, and have rebelled, even by departing from thy precepts and from thy judgments: 6 Neither have we hearkened unto thy servants the prophets, which spake in thy name to our kings, our princes, and our fathers, and to all the people of the land. 7 O Lord, righteousness belongeth unto thee, but unto us confusion of faces, as at this day; to the men of Judah, and to the inhabitants of Jerusalem, and unto all Israel, that are near, and that are far off, through all the countries whither thou hast driven them, because of their trespass that they have trespassed against thee. 8

Visit TimeToFreeAmerica.com/TheHomoDeuce to watch the video clips referenced throughout this book.

O Lord, to us belongeth confusion of face, to our kings, to our princes, and to our fathers, because we have sinned against thee. 9 To the Lord our God belong mercies and forgivenesses, though we have rebelled against him; 10 Neither have we obeyed the voice of the LORD our God, to walk in his laws, which he set before us by his servants the prophets. 11 Yea, all Israel have transgressed thy law, even by departing, that they might not obey thy voice; therefore the curse is poured upon us, and the oath that is written in the law of Moses the servant of God, because we have sinned against him. 12 And he hath confirmed his words, which he spake against us, and against our judges that judged us, by bringing upon us a great evil: for under the whole heaven hath not been done as hath been done upon Jerusalem. 13 As it is written in the law of Moses, all this evil is come upon us: yet made we not our prayer before the LORD our God, that we might turn from our iniquities, and understand thy truth. 14 Therefore hath the LORD watched upon the evil, and brought it upon us: for the LORD our God is righteous in all his works which he doeth: for we obeyed not his voice. 15 And now, O Lord our God, that hast brought thy people forth out of the land of Egypt with a mighty hand, and hast gotten thee renown, as at this day; we have sinned, we have done wickedly. 16 O Lord, according to all thy righteousness, I beseech thee, let thine anger and thy fury be turned away

Visit TimeToFreeAmerica.com/TheHomoDeuce to watch the video clips referenced throughout this book.

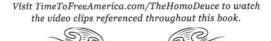

from thy city Jerusalem, thy holy mountain: because for our sins, and for the iniquities of our fathers, Jerusalem and thy people are become a reproach to all that are about us. 17 Now therefore, O our God, hear the prayer of thy servant, and his supplications, and cause thy face to shine upon thy sanctuary that is desolate, for the Lord's sake. 18 O my God, incline thine ear, and hear; open thine eyes, and behold our desolations, and the city which is called by thy name: for we do not present our supplications before thee for our righteousnesses, but for thy great mercies. 19 O Lord, hear; O Lord, forgive; O Lord, hearken and do; defer not, for thine own sake, O my God: for thy city and thy people are called by thy name. 20 And whiles I was speaking, and praying, and confessing my sin and the sin of my people Israel, and presenting my supplication before the LORD my God for the holy mountain of my God; 21 Yea, whiles I was speaking in prayer, even the man Gabriel, whom I had seen in the vision at the beginning, being caused to fly swiftly, touched me about the time of the evening oblation. 22 And he informed me, and talked with me, and said, O Daniel, I am now come forth to give thee skill and understanding. 23 At the beginning of thy supplications the commandment came forth, and I am come to shew thee; for thou art greatly beloved: therefore understand the matter, and consider the vision. 24 Seventy weeks are determined upon thy people and upon thy holy

Visit TimeToFreeAmerica.com/TheHomoDeuce to watch
the video clips referenced throughout this book.

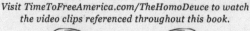

city, to finish the transgression, and to make an end of sins, and to make reconciliation for iniquity, and to bring in everlasting righteousness, and to seal up the vision and prophecy, and to anoint the most Holy. 25 Know therefore and understand, that from the going forth of the commandment to restore and to build Jerusalem unto the Messiah the Prince shall be seven weeks, and threescore and two weeks: the street shall be built again, and the wall, even in troublous times. 26 And after threescore and two weeks shall Messiah be cut off, but not for himself: and the people of the prince that shall come shall destroy the city and the sanctuary; and the end thereof shall be with a flood, and unto the end of the war desolations are determined. 27 And he shall confirm the covenant with many for one week: and in the midst of the week he shall cause the sacrifice and the oblation to cease, and for the overspreading of abominations he shall make it desolate, even until the consummation, and that determined shall be poured upon the desolate.

CHAPTER 10

1 In the third year of Cyrus king of Persia a thing was revealed unto Daniel, whose name was called Belteshazzar; and the thing was true, but the time appointed was long:

Visit TimeToFreeAmerica.com/TheHomoDeuce to watch
the video clips referenced throughout this book.

and he understood the thing, and had understanding of the vision. 2 In those days I Daniel was mourning three full weeks. 3 I ate no pleasant bread, neither came flesh nor wine in my mouth, neither did I anoint myself at all, till three whole weeks were fulfilled. 4 And in the four and twentieth day of the first month, as I was by the side of the great river, which is Hiddekel; 5 Then I lifted up mine eyes, and looked, and behold a certain man clothed in linen, whose loins were girded with fine gold of Uphaz: 6 His body also was like the beryl, and his face as the appearance of lightning, and his eyes as lamps of fire, and his arms and his feet like in colour to polished brass, and the voice of his words like the voice of a multitude. 7 And I Daniel alone saw the vision: for the men that were with me saw not the vision; but a great quaking fell upon them, so that they fled to hide themselves. 8 Therefore I was left alone, and saw this great vision, and there remained no strength in me: for my comeliness was turned in me into corruption, and I retained no strength. 9 Yet heard I the voice of his words: and when I heard the voice of his words, then was I in a deep sleep on my face, and my face toward the ground. 10 And, behold, an hand touched me, which set me upon my knees and upon the palms of my hands. 11 And he said unto me, O Daniel, a man greatly beloved, understand the words that I speak unto thee, and stand upright: for unto thee am I now sent. And when he had spoken this word

Visit TimeToFreeAmerica.com/TheHomoDeuce to watch the video clips referenced throughout this book.

unto me, I stood trembling. 12 Then said he unto me, Fear not, Daniel: for from the first day that thou didst set thine heart to understand, and to chasten thyself before thy God, thy words were heard, and I am come for thy words. 13 But the prince of the kingdom of Persia withstood me one and twenty days: but, lo, Michael, one of the chief princes, came to help me; and I remained there with the kings of Persia. 14 Now I am come to make thee understand what shall befall thy people in the latter days: for yet the vision is for many days. 15 And when he had spoken such words unto me, I set my face toward the ground, and I became dumb. 16 And, behold, one like the similitude of the sons of men touched my lips: then I opened my mouth, and spake, and said unto him that stood before me, O my lord, by the vision my sorrows are turned upon me, and I have retained no strength. 17 For how can the servant of this my lord talk with this my lord? for as for me, straightway there remained no strength in me, neither is there breath left in me. 18 Then there came again and touched me one like the appearance of a man, and he strengthened me, 19 And said, O man greatly beloved, fear not: peace be unto thee, be strong, yea, be strong. And when he had spoken unto me, I was strengthened, and said, Let my lord speak; for thou hast strengthened me. 20 Then said he, Knowest thou wherefore I come unto thee? and now will I return to fight with the prince of Persia: and when I am gone forth,

Visit *TimeToFreeAmerica.com/TheHomoDeuce* to watch the video clips referenced throughout this book.

lo, the prince of Grecia shall come. 21 But I will shew thee that which is noted in the scripture of truth: and there is none that holdeth with me in these things, but Michael your prince.

CHAPTER 11

1 Also I in the first year of Darius the Mede, even I, stood to confirm and to strengthen him. 2 And now will I shew thee the truth. Behold, there shall stand up yet three kings in Persia; and the fourth shall be far richer than they all: and by his strength through his riches he shall stir up all against the realm of Grecia. 3 And a mighty king shall stand up, that shall rule with great dominion, and do according to his will. 4 And when he shall stand up, his kingdom shall be broken, and shall be divided toward the four winds of heaven; and not to his posterity, nor according to his dominion which he ruled: for his kingdom shall be plucked up, even for others beside those. 5 And the king of the south shall be strong, and one of his princes; and he shall be strong above him, and have dominion; his dominion shall be a great dominion. 6 And in the end of years they shall join themselves together; for the king's daughter of the south shall come to the king of the north to make an agreement: but she shall not retain the power of

Visit *TimeToFreeAmerica.com/TheHomoDeuce* to watch the video clips referenced throughout this book.

the arm; neither shall he stand, nor his arm: but she shall be given up, and they that brought her, and he that begat her, and he that strengthened her in these times. 7 But out of a branch of her roots shall one stand up in his estate, which shall come with an army, and shall enter into the fortress of the king of the north, and shall deal against them, and shall prevail: 8 And shall also carry captives into Egypt their gods, with their princes, and with their precious vessels of silver and of gold; and he shall continue more years than the king of the north. 9 So the king of the south shall come into his kingdom, and shall return into his own land. 10 But his sons shall be stirred up, and shall assemble a multitude of great forces: and one shall certainly come, and overflow, and pass through: then shall he return, and be stirred up, even to his fortress. 11 And the king of the south shall be moved with choler, and shall come forth and fight with him, even with the king of the north: and he shall set forth a great multitude; but the multitude shall be given into his hand. 12 And when he hath taken away the multitude, his heart shall be lifted up; and he shall cast down many ten thousands: but he shall not be strengthened by it. 13 For the king of the north shall return, and shall set forth a multitude greater than the former, and shall certainly come after certain years with a great army and with much riches. 14 And in those times there shall many stand up against the king of the south: also the robbers of

Visit *TimeToFreeAmerica.com/TheHomoDeuce* to watch
the video clips referenced throughout this book.

thy people shall exalt themselves to establish the vision; but they shall fall. 15 So the king of the north shall come, and cast up a mount, and take the most fenced cities: and the arms of the south shall not withstand, neither his chosen people, neither shall there be any strength to withstand. 16 But he that cometh against him shall do according to his own will, and none shall stand before him: and he shall stand in the glorious land, which by his hand shall be consumed. 17 He shall also set his face to enter with the strength of his whole kingdom, and upright ones with him; thus shall he do: and he shall give him the daughter of women, corrupting her: but she shall not stand on his side, neither be for him. 18 After this shall he turn his face unto the isles, and shall take many: but a prince for his own behalf shall cause the reproach offered by him to cease; without his own reproach he shall cause it to turn upon him. 19 Then he shall turn his face toward the fort of his own land: but he shall stumble and fall, and not be found. 20 Then shall stand up in his estate a raiser of taxes in the glory of the kingdom: but within few days he shall be destroyed, neither in anger, nor in battle. 21 And in his estate shall stand up a vile person, to whom they shall not give the honour of the kingdom: but he shall come in peaceably, and obtain the kingdom by flatteries. 22 And with the arms of a flood shall they be overflown from before him, and shall be broken; yea, also the prince of the

Visit *TimeToFreeAmerica.com/TheHomoDeuce* to watch
the video clips referenced throughout this book.

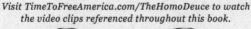

covenant. 23 And after the league made with him he shall work deceitfully: for he shall come up, and shall become strong with a small people. 24 He shall enter peaceably even upon the fattest places of the province; and he shall do that which his fathers have not done, nor his fathers' fathers; he shall scatter among them the prey, and spoil, and riches: yea, and he shall forecast his devices against the strong holds, even for a time. 25 And he shall stir up his power and his courage against the king of the south with a great army; and the king of the south shall be stirred up to battle with a very great and mighty army; but he shall not stand: for they shall forecast devices against him. 26 Yea, they that feed of the portion of his meat shall destroy him, and his army shall overflow: and many shall fall down slain. 27 And both these kings' hearts shall be to do mischief, and they shall speak lies at one table; but it shall not prosper: for yet the end shall be at the time appointed. 28 Then shall he return into his land with great riches; and his heart shall be against the holy covenant; and he shall do exploits, and return to his own land. 29 At the time appointed he shall return, and come toward the south; but it shall not be as the former, or as the latter. 30 For the ships of Chittim shall come against him: therefore he shall be grieved, and return, and have indignation against the holy covenant: so shall he do; he shall even return, and have intelligence with them that forsake the holy covenant.

Visit *TimeToFreeAmerica.com/TheHomoDeuce* to watch
the video clips referenced throughout this book.

31 And arms shall stand on his part, and they shall pollute the sanctuary of strength, and shall take away the daily sacrifice, and they shall place the abomination that maketh desolate. 32 And such as do wickedly against the covenant shall he corrupt by flatteries: but the people that do know their God shall be strong, and do exploits. 33 And they that understand among the people shall instruct many: yet they shall fall by the sword, and by flame, by captivity, and by spoil, many days. 34 Now when they shall fall, they shall be holpen with a little help: but many shall cleave to them with flatteries. 35 And some of them of understanding shall fall, to try them, and to purge, and to make them white, even to the time of the end: because it is yet for a time appointed. 36 And the king shall do according to his will; and he shall exalt himself, and magnify himself above every god, and shall speak marvellous things against the God of gods, and shall prosper till the indignation be accomplished: for that that is determined shall be done. 37 Neither shall he regard the God of his fathers, nor the desire of women, nor regard any god: for he shall magnify himself above all. 38 But in his estate shall he honour the God of forces: and a god whom his fathers knew not shall he honour with gold, and silver, and with precious stones, and pleasant things. 39 Thus shall he do in the most strong holds with a strange god, whom he shall acknowledge and increase with glory: and he shall cause them to rule over

Visit *TimeToFreeAmerica.com/TheHomoDeuce* to watch
the video clips referenced throughout this book.

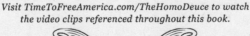

many, and shall divide the land for gain. 40 And at the time of the end shall the king of the south push at him: and the king of the north shall come against him like a whirlwind, with chariots, and with horsemen, and with many ships; and he shall enter into the countries, and shall overflow and pass over. 41 He shall enter also into the glorious land, and many countries shall be overthrown: but these shall escape out of his hand, even Edom, and Moab, and the chief of the children of Ammon. 42 He shall stretch forth his hand also upon the countries: and the land of Egypt shall not escape. 43 But he shall have power over the treasures of gold and of silver, and over all the precious things of Egypt: and the Libyans and the Ethiopians shall be at his steps. 44 But tidings out of the east and out of the north shall trouble him: therefore he shall go forth with great fury to destroy, and utterly to make away many. 45 And he shall plant the tabernacles of his palace between the seas in the glorious holy mountain; yet he shall come to his end, and none shall help him.

CHAPTER 12

1 And at that time shall Michael stand up, the great prince which standeth for the children of thy people: and there shall be a time of trouble, such as never was since

Visit *TimeToFreeAmerica.com/TheHomoDeuce* to watch
the video clips referenced throughout this book.

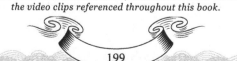

there was a nation even to that same time: and at that time thy people shall be delivered, every one that shall be found written in the book. 2 And many of them that sleep in the dust of the earth shall awake, some to everlasting life, and some to shame and everlasting contempt. 3 And they that be wise shall shine as the brightness of the firmament; and they that turn many to righteousness as the stars for ever and ever. 4 But thou, O Daniel, shut up the words, and seal the book, even to the time of the end: many shall run to and fro, and knowledge shall be increased. 5 Then I Daniel looked, and, behold, there stood other two, the one on this side of the bank of the river, and the other on that side of the bank of the river. 6 And one said to the man clothed in linen, which was upon the waters of the river, How long shall it be to the end of these wonders? 7 And I heard the man clothed in linen, which was upon the waters of the river, when he held up his right hand and his left hand unto heaven, and sware by him that liveth for ever that it shall be for a time, times, and an half; and when he shall have accomplished to scatter the power of the holy people, all these things shall be finished. 8 And I heard, but I understood not: then said I, O my Lord, what shall be the end of these things? 9 And he said, Go thy way, Daniel: for the words are closed up and sealed till the time of the end. 10 Many shall be purified, and made white, and tried; but the wicked shall do wickedly: and none of the

Visit TimeToFreeAmerica.com/TheHomoDeuce to watch the video clips referenced throughout this book.

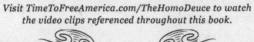

wicked shall understand; but the wise shall understand. 11 And from the time that the daily sacrifice shall be taken away, and the abomination that maketh desolate set up, there shall be a thousand two hundred and ninety days. 12 Blessed is he that waiteth, and cometh to the thousand three hundred and five and thirty days. 13 But go thou thy way till the end be: for thou shalt rest, and stand in thy lot at the end of the days.

Visit TimeToFreeAmerica.com/TheHomoDeuce to watch the video clips referenced throughout this book.

The Book of
St. Matthew
- Chapter 24

*Visit TimeToFreeAmerica.com/TheHomoDeuce to watch
the video clips referenced throughout this book.*

MATTHEW - CHAPTER 24

1 And Jesus went out, and departed from the temple: and his disciples came to him for to shew him the buildings of the temple. 2 And Jesus said unto them, See ye not all these things? verily I say unto you, There shall not be left here one stone upon another, that shall not be thrown down. 3 And as he sat upon the mount of Olives, the disciples came unto him privately, saying, Tell us, when shall these things be? and what shall be the sign of thy coming, and of the end of the world? 4 And Jesus answered and said unto them, Take heed that no man deceive you. 5 For many shall come in my name, saying, I am Christ; and shall deceive many. 6 And ye shall hear of wars and rumours of wars: see that ye be not troubled: for all these things must come to pass, but the end is not yet. 7 For nation shall rise against nation, and kingdom against kingdom: and there shall be famines, and pestilences, and earthquakes, in divers places. 8 All these are the beginning of sorrows. 9 Then shall they deliver you up to be afflicted, and shall kill you: and ye shall be hated of all nations for my name's sake. 10 And then shall many be offended, and shall betray one another, and shall hate one another. 11 And many false prophets shall rise, and shall deceive many. 12 And because iniquity shall abound, the love of many shall wax cold. 13 But he that shall endure

Visit TimeToFreeAmerica.com/TheHomoDeuce to watch the video clips referenced throughout this book.

unto the end, the same shall be saved. 14 And this gospel of the kingdom shall be preached in all the world for a witness unto all nations; and then shall the end come. 15 When ye therefore shall see the abomination of desolation, spoken of by Daniel the prophet, stand in the holy place, (whoso readeth, let him understand:) 16 Then let them which be in Judaea flee into the mountains: 17 Let him which is on the housetop not come down to take any thing out of his house: 18 Neither let him which is in the field return back to take his clothes. 19 And woe unto them that are with child, and to them that give suck in those days! 20 But pray ye that your flight be not in the winter, neither on the sabbath day: 21 For then shall be great tribulation, such as was not since the beginning of the world to this time, no, nor ever shall be. 22 And except those days should be shortened, there should no flesh be saved: but for the elect's sake those days shall be shortened. 23 Then if any man shall say unto you, Lo, here is Christ, or there; believe it not. 24 For there shall arise false Christs, and false prophets, and shall shew great signs and wonders; insomuch that, if it were possible, they shall deceive the very elect. 25 Behold, I have told you before. 26 Wherefore if they shall say unto you, Behold, he is in the desert; go not forth: behold, he is in the secret chambers; believe it not. 27 For as the lightning cometh out of the east, and shineth even unto the west; so shall also the coming of the Son of man be. 28 For wheresoever

Visit *TimeToFreeAmerica.com/TheHomoDeuce* to watch
the video clips referenced throughout this book.

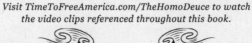

the carcase is, there will the eagles be gathered together. 29 Immediately after the tribulation of those days shall the sun be darkened, and the moon shall not give her light, and the stars shall fall from heaven, and the powers of the heavens shall be shaken: 30 And then shall appear the sign of the Son of man in heaven: and then shall all the tribes of the earth mourn, and they shall see the Son of man coming in the clouds of heaven with power and great glory. 31 And he shall send his angels with a great sound of a trumpet, and they shall gather together his elect from the four winds, from one end of heaven to the other. 32 Now learn a parable of the fig tree; When his branch is yet tender, and putteth forth leaves, ye know that summer is nigh: 33 So likewise ye, when ye shall see all these things, know that it is near, even at the doors. 34 Verily I say unto you, This generation shall not pass, till all these things be fulfilled. 35 Heaven and earth shall pass away, but my words shall not pass away. 36 But of that day and hour knoweth no man, no, not the angels of heaven, but my Father only. 37 But as the days of Noe were, so shall also the coming of the Son of man be. 38 For as in the days that were before the flood they were eating and drinking, marrying and giving in marriage, until the day that Noe entered into the ark, 39 And knew not until the flood came, and took them all away; so shall also the coming of the Son of man be. 40 Then shall two be in the field; the one shall be taken, and the

Visit *TimeToFreeAmerica.com/TheHomoDeuce* to watch the video clips referenced throughout this book.

other left. 41 Two women shall be grinding at the mill; the one shall be taken, and the other left. 42 Watch therefore: for ye know not what hour your Lord doth come. 43 But know this, that if the goodman of the house had known in what watch the thief would come, he would have watched, and would not have suffered his house to be broken up. 44 Therefore be ye also ready: for in such an hour as ye think not the Son of man cometh. 45 Who then is a faithful and wise servant, whom his lord hath made ruler over his household, to give them meat in due season? 46 Blessed is that servant, whom his lord when he cometh shall find so doing. 47 Verily I say unto you, That he shall make him ruler over all his goods. 48 But and if that evil servant shall say in his heart, My lord delayeth his coming; 49 And shall begin to smite his fellowservants, and to eat and drink with the drunken; 50 The lord of that servant shall come in a day when he looketh not for him, and in an hour that he is not aware of, 51 And shall cut him asunder, and appoint him his portion with the hypocrites: there shall be weeping and gnashing of teeth.

Visit *TimeToFreeAmerica.com/TheHomoDeuce* to watch
the video clips referenced throughout this book.

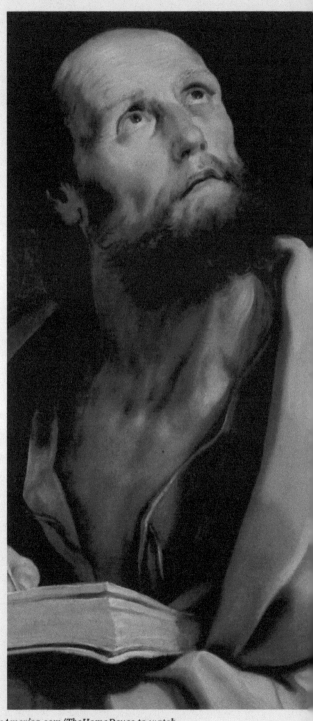

Visit *TimeToFreeAmerica.com/TheHomoDeuce to watch*
the video clips referenced throughout this book.

LUKE - CHAPTER 9

1 Then he called his twelve disciples together, and gave them power and authority over all devils, and to cure diseases. 2 And he sent them to preach the kingdom of God, and to heal the sick. 3 And he said unto them, Take nothing for your journey, neither staves, nor scrip, neither bread, neither money; neither have two coats apiece. 4 And whatsoever house ye enter into, there abide, and thence depart. 5 And whosoever will not receive you, when ye go out of that city, shake off the very dust from your feet for a testimony against them. 6 And they departed, and went through the towns, preaching the gospel, and healing every where. 7 Now Herod the tetrarch heard of all that was done by him: and he was perplexed, because that it was said of some, that John was risen from the dead; 8 And of some, that Elias had appeared; and of others, that one of the old prophets was risen again. 9 And Herod said, John have I beheaded: but who is this, of whom I hear such things? And he desired to see him. 10 And the apostles, when they were returned, told him all that they had done. And he took them, and went aside privately into a desert place belonging to the city called Bethsaida. 11 And the people, when they knew it, followed him: and he received them, and spake unto them of the kingdom of God, and healed

Visit *TimeToFreeAmerica.com/TheHomoDeuce* to watch the video clips referenced throughout this book.

them that had need of healing. 12 And when the day began to wear away, then came the twelve, and said unto him, Send the multitude away, that they may go into the towns and country round about, and lodge, and get victuals: for we are here in a desert place. 13 But he said unto them, Give ye them to eat. And they said, We have no more but five loaves and two fishes; except we should go and buy meat for all this people. 14 For they were about five thousand men. And he said to his disciples, Make them sit down by fifties in a company. 15 And they did so, and made them all sit down. 16 Then he took the five loaves and the two fishes, and looking up to heaven, he blessed them, and brake, and gave to the disciples to set before the multitude. 17 And they did eat, and were all filled: and there was taken up of fragments that remained to them twelve baskets. 18 And it came to pass, as he was alone praying, his disciples were with him: and he asked them, saying, Whom say the people that I am? 19 They answering said, John the Baptist; but some say, Elias; and others say, that one of the old prophets is risen again. 20 He said unto them, But whom say ye that I am? Peter answering said, The Christ of God. 21 And he straitly charged them, and commanded them to tell no man that thing; 22 Saying, The Son of man must suffer many things, and be rejected of the elders and chief priests and scribes, and be slain, and be raised the third day. 23 And he said to them all, If

Visit *TimeToFreeAmerica.com/TheHomoDeuce* to watch
the video clips referenced throughout this book.

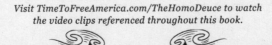

any man will come after me, let him deny himself, and take up his cross daily, and follow me. 24 For whosoever will save his life shall lose it: but whosoever will lose his life for my sake, the same shall save it. 25 For what is a man advantaged, if he gain the whole world, and lose himself, or be cast away? 26 For whosoever shall be ashamed of me and of my words, of him shall the Son of man be ashamed, when he shall come in his own glory, and in his Father's, and of the holy angels. 27 But I tell you of a truth, there be some standing here, which shall not taste of death, till they see the kingdom of God. 28 And it came to pass about an eight days after these sayings, he took Peter and John and James, and went up into a mountain to pray. 29 And as he prayed, the fashion of his countenance was altered, and his raiment was white and glistering. 30 And, behold, there talked with him two men, which were Moses and Elias: 31 Who appeared in glory, and spake of his decease which he should accomplish at Jerusalem. 32 But Peter and they that were with him were heavy with sleep: and when they were awake, they saw his glory, and the two men that stood with him. 33 And it came to pass, as they departed from him, Peter said unto Jesus, Master, it is good for us to be here: and let us make three tabernacles; one for thee, and one for Moses, and one for Elias: not knowing what he said. 34 While he thus spake, there came a cloud, and overshadowed them: and they feared as they

Visit *TimeToFreeAmerica.com/TheHomoDeuce* to watch the video clips referenced throughout this book.

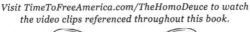

entered into the cloud. 35 And there came a voice out of the cloud, saying, This is my beloved Son: hear him. 36 And when the voice was past, Jesus was found alone. And they kept it close, and told no man in those days any of those things which they had seen. 37 And it came to pass, that on the next day, when they were come down from the hill, much people met him. 38 And, behold, a man of the company cried out, saying, Master, I beseech thee, look upon my son: for he is mine only child. 39 And, lo, a spirit taketh him, and he suddenly crieth out; and it teareth him that he foameth again, and bruising him hardly departeth from him. 40 And I besought thy disciples to cast him out; and they could not. 41 And Jesus answering said, O faithless and perverse generation, how long shall I be with you, and suffer you? Bring thy son hither. 42 And as he was yet a coming, the devil threw him down, and tare him. And Jesus rebuked the unclean spirit, and healed the child, and delivered him again to his father. 43 And they were all amazed at the mighty power of God. But while they wondered every one at all things which Jesus did, he said unto his disciples, 44 Let these sayings sink down into your ears: for the Son of man shall be delivered into the hands of men. 45 But they understood not this saying, and it was hid from them, that they perceived it not: and they feared to ask him of that saying. 46 Then there arose a reasoning among them, which of them should be greatest.

Visit TimeToFreeAmerica.com/TheHomoDeuce to watch
the video clips referenced throughout this book.

47 And Jesus, perceiving the thought of their heart, took a child, and set him by him, 48 And said unto them, Whosoever shall receive this child in my name receiveth me: and whosoever shall receive me receiveth him that sent me: for he that is least among you all, the same shall be great. 49 And John answered and said, Master, we saw one casting out devils in thy name; and we forbad him, because he followeth not with us. 50 And Jesus said unto him, Forbid him not: for he that is not against us is for us. 51 And it came to pass, when the time was come that he should be received up, he stedfastly set his face to go to Jerusalem, 52 And sent messengers before his face: and they went, and entered into a village of the Samaritans, to make ready for him. 53 And they did not receive him, because his face was as though he would go to Jerusalem. 54 And when his disciples James and John saw this, they said, Lord, wilt thou that we command fire to come down from heaven, and consume them, even as Elias did? 55 But he turned, and rebuked them, and said, Ye know not what manner of spirit ye are of. 56 For the Son of man is not come to destroy men's lives, but to save them. And they went to another village. 57 And it came to pass, that, as they went in the way, a certain man said unto him, Lord, I will follow thee whithersoever thou goest. 58 And Jesus said unto him, Foxes have holes, and birds of the air have nests; but the Son of man hath not where to lay his head.

Visit TimeToFreeAmerica.com/TheHomoDeuce to watch the video clips referenced throughout this book.

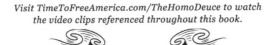

59 And he said unto another, Follow me. But he said, Lord, suffer me first to go and bury my father. 60 Jesus said unto him, Let the dead bury their dead: but go thou and preach the kingdom of God. 61 And another also said, Lord, I will follow thee; but let me first go bid them farewell, which are at home at my house. 62 And Jesus said unto him, No man, having put his hand to the plough, and looking back, is fit for the kingdom of God.

LUKE - CHAPTER 21

1 And he looked up, and saw the rich men casting their gifts into the treasury. 2 And he saw also a certain poor widow casting in thither two mites. 3 And he said, Of a truth I say unto you, that this poor widow hath cast in more than they all: 4 For all these have of their abundance cast in unto the offerings of God: but she of her penury hath cast in all the living that she had. 5 And as some spake of the temple, how it was adorned with goodly stones and gifts, he said, 6 As for these things which ye behold, the days will come, in the which there shall not be left one stone upon another, that shall not be thrown down. 7 And they asked him, saying, Master, but when shall these things be? and what sign will there be when these things shall come to pass? 8 And he said, Take heed that ye be not deceived:

Visit TimeToFreeAmerica.com/TheHomoDeuce to watch the video clips referenced throughout this book.

for many shall come in my name, saying, I am Christ; and the time draweth near: go ye not therefore after them. 9 But when ye shall hear of wars and commotions, be not terrified: for these things must first come to pass; but the end is not by and by. 10 Then said he unto them, Nation shall rise against nation, and kingdom against kingdom: 11 And great earthquakes shall be in divers places, and famines, and pestilences; and fearful sights and great signs shall there be from heaven. 12 But before all these, they shall lay their hands on you, and persecute you, delivering you up to the synagogues, and into prisons, being brought before kings and rulers for my name's sake. 13 And it shall turn to you for a testimony. 14 Settle it therefore in your hearts, not to meditate before what ye shall answer: 15 For I will give you a mouth and wisdom, which all your adversaries shall not be able to gainsay nor resist. 16 And ye shall be betrayed both by parents, and brethren, and kinsfolks, and friends; and some of you shall they cause to be put to death. 17 And ye shall be hated of all men for my name's sake. 18 But there shall not an hair of your head perish. 19 In your patience possess ye your souls. 20 And when ye shall see Jerusalem compassed with armies, then know that the desolation thereof is nigh. 21 Then let them which are in Judaea flee to the mountains; and let them which are in the midst of it depart out; and let not them that are in the countries enter thereinto. 22 For these be

Visit *TimeToFreeAmerica.com/TheHomoDeuce* to watch
the video clips referenced throughout this book.

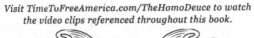

the days of vengeance, that all things which are written may be fulfilled. 23 But woe unto them that are with child, and to them that give suck, in those days! for there shall be great distress in the land, and wrath upon this people. 24 And they shall fall by the edge of the sword, and shall be led away captive into all nations: and Jerusalem shall be trodden down of the Gentiles, until the times of the Gentiles be fulfilled. 25 And there shall be signs in the sun, and in the moon, and in the stars; and upon the earth distress of nations, with perplexity; the sea and the waves roaring; 26 Men's hearts failing them for fear, and for looking after those things which are coming on the earth: for the powers of heaven shall be shaken. 27 And then shall they see the Son of man coming in a cloud with power and great glory. 28 And when these things begin to come to pass, then look up, and lift up your heads; for your redemption draweth nigh. 29 And he spake to them a parable; Behold the fig tree, and all the trees; 30 When they now shoot forth, ye see and know of your own selves that summer is now nigh at hand. 31 So likewise ye, when ye see these things come to pass, know ye that the kingdom of God is nigh at hand. 32 Verily I say unto you, This generation shall not pass away, till all be fulfilled. 33 Heaven and earth shall pass away: but my words shall not pass away. 34 And take heed to yourselves, lest at any time your hearts be overcharged with surfeiting, and drunkenness, and cares of this life,

Visit TimeToFreeAmerica.com/TheHomoDeuce to watch
the video clips referenced throughout this book.

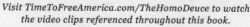

and so that day come upon you unawares. 35 For as a snare shall it come on all them that dwell on the face of the whole earth. 36 Watch ye therefore, and pray always, that ye may be accounted worthy to escape all these things that shall come to pass, and to stand before the Son of man. 37 And in the day time he was teaching in the temple; and at night he went out, and abode in the mount that is called the mount of Olives. 38 And all the people came early in the morning to him in the temple, for to hear him.

Visit TimeToFreeAmerica.com/TheHomoDeuce to watch
the video clips referenced throughout this book.

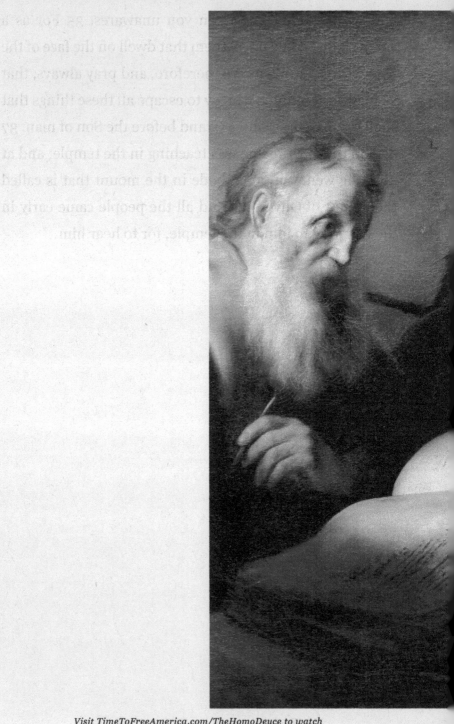

Visit *TimeToFreeAmerica.com/TheHomoDeuce* to watch
the video clips referenced throughout this book.

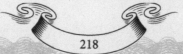

II Thessalonians - Chapter 2

2 Now we beseech you, brethren, by the coming of our Lord Jesus Christ, and by our gathering together unto him, 2 That ye be not soon shaken in mind, or be troubled, neither by spirit, nor by word, nor by letter as from us, as that the day of Christ is at hand. 3 Let no man deceive you by any means: for that day shall not come, except there come a falling away first, and that man of sin be revealed, the son of perdition; 4 Who opposeth and exalteth himself above all that is called God, or that is worshipped; so that he as God sitteth in the temple of God, shewing himself that he is God. 5 Remember ye not, that, when I was yet with you, I told you these things? 6 And now ye know what withholdeth that he might be revealed in his time. 7 For the mystery of iniquity doth already work: only he who now letteth will let, until he be taken out of the way. 8 And then shall that Wicked be revealed, whom the Lord shall consume with the spirit of his mouth, and shall destroy with the brightness of his coming: 9 Even him, whose coming is after the working of Satan with all power and signs and lying wonders, 10 And with all deceivableness of unrighteousness in them that perish; because they received not the love of the truth, that they might be saved. 11 And for this cause God shall send them strong delusion,

Visit TimeToFreeAmerica.com/TheHomoDeuce to watch the video clips referenced throughout this book.

that they should believe a lie: 12 That they all might be damned who believed not the truth, but had pleasure in unrighteousness. 13 But we are bound to give thanks alway to God for you, brethren beloved of the Lord, because God hath from the beginning chosen you to salvation through sanctification of the Spirit and belief of the truth: 14 Whereunto he called you by our gospel, to the obtaining of the glory of our Lord Jesus Christ. 15 Therefore, brethren, stand fast, and hold the traditions which ye have been taught, whether by word, or our epistle. 16 Now our Lord Jesus Christ himself, and God, even our Father, which hath loved us, and hath given us everlasting consolation and good hope through grace, 17 Comfort your hearts, and stablish you in every good word and work.

Visit TimeToFreeAmerica.com/TheHomoDeuce to watch the video clips referenced throughout this book.

220

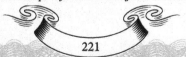

The Book of Revelation

Visit TimeToFreeAmerica.com/TheHomoDeuce to watch
the video clips referenced throughout this book.

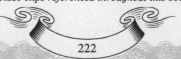

CHAPTER 1

1 The Revelation of Jesus Christ, which God gave unto him, to shew unto his servants things which must shortly come to pass; and he sent and signified it by his angel unto his servant John: 2 Who bare record of the word of God, and of the testimony of Jesus Christ, and of all things that he saw. 3 Blessed is he that readeth, and they that hear the words of this prophecy, and keep those things which are written therein: for the time is at hand. 4 John to the seven churches which are in Asia: Grace be unto you, and peace, from him which is, and which was, and which is to come; and from the seven Spirits which are before his throne; 5 And from Jesus Christ, who is the faithful witness, and the first begotten of the dead, and the prince of the kings of the earth. Unto him that loved us, and washed us from our sins in his own blood, 6 And hath made us kings and priests unto God and his Father; to him be glory and dominion for ever and ever. Amen. 7 Behold, he cometh with clouds; and every eye shall see him, and they also which pierced him: and all kindreds of the earth shall wail because of him. Even so, Amen. 8 I am Alpha and Omega, the beginning and the ending, saith the Lord, which is, and which was, and which is to come, the Almighty. 9 I John, who also am your brother, and companion in tribulation, and in the kingdom

Visit TimeToFreeAmerica.com/TheHomoDeuce to watch the video clips referenced throughout this book.

and patience of Jesus Christ, was in the isle that is called Patmos, for the word of God, and for the testimony of Jesus Christ. 10 I was in the Spirit on the Lord's day, and heard behind me a great voice, as of a trumpet, 11 Saying, I am Alpha and Omega, the first and the last: and, What thou seest, write in a book, and send it unto the seven churches which are in Asia; unto Ephesus, and unto Smyrna, and unto Pergamos, and unto Thyatira, and unto Sardis, and unto Philadelphia, and unto Laodicea. 12 And I turned to see the voice that spake with me. And being turned, I saw seven golden candlesticks; 13 And in the midst of the seven candlesticks one like unto the Son of man, clothed with a garment down to the foot, and girt about the paps with a golden girdle. 14 His head and his hairs were white like wool, as white as snow; and his eyes were as a flame of fire; 15 And his feet like unto fine brass, as if they burned in a furnace; and his voice as the sound of many waters. 16 And he had in his right hand seven stars: and out of his mouth went a sharp twoedged sword: and his countenance was as the sun shineth in his strength. 17 And when I saw him, I fell at his feet as dead. And he laid his right hand upon me, saying unto me, Fear not; I am the first and the last: 18 I am he that liveth, and was dead; and, behold, I am alive for evermore, Amen; and have the keys of hell and of death. 19 Write the things which thou hast seen, and the things which are, and the things which shall be hereafter;

Visit TimeToFreeAmerica.com/TheHomoDeuce to watch
the video clips referenced throughout this book.

20 The mystery of the seven stars which thou sawest in my right hand, and the seven golden candlesticks. The seven stars are the angels of the seven churches: and the seven candlesticks which thou sawest are the seven churches.

CHAPTER 2

1 Unto the angel of the church of Ephesus write; These things saith he that holdeth the seven stars in his right hand, who walketh in the midst of the seven golden candlesticks; 2 I know thy works, and thy labour, and thy patience, and how thou canst not bear them which are evil: and thou hast tried them which say they are apostles, and are not, and hast found them liars: 3 And hast borne, and hast patience, and for my name's sake hast laboured, and hast not fainted. 4 Nevertheless I have somewhat against thee, because thou hast left thy first love. 5 Remember therefore from whence thou art fallen, and repent, and do the first works; or else I will come unto thee quickly, and will remove thy candlestick out of his place, except thou repent. 6 But this thou hast, that thou hatest the deeds of the Nicolaitans, which I also hate. 7 He that hath an ear, let him hear what the Spirit saith unto the churches; To him that overcometh will I give to eat of the tree of life, which is in the midst of the paradise of God. 8 And unto the angel of

Visit TimeToFreeAmerica.com/TheHomoDeuce to watch
the video clips referenced throughout this book.

the church in Smyrna write; These things saith the first and the last, which was dead, and is alive; 9 I know thy works, and tribulation, and poverty, (but thou art rich) and I know the blasphemy of them which say they are Jews, and are not, but are the synagogue of Satan. 10 Fear none of those things which thou shalt suffer: behold, the devil shall cast some of you into prison, that ye may be tried; and ye shall have tribulation ten days: be thou faithful unto death, and I will give thee a crown of life. 11 He that hath an ear, let him hear what the Spirit saith unto the churches; He that overcometh shall not be hurt of the second death. 12 And to the angel of the church in Pergamos write; These things saith he which hath the sharp sword with two edges; 13 I know thy works, and where thou dwellest, even where Satan's seat is: and thou holdest fast my name, and hast not denied my faith, even in those days wherein Antipas was my faithful martyr, who was slain among you, where Satan dwelleth. 14 But I have a few things against thee, because thou hast there them that hold the doctrine of Balaam, who taught Balac to cast a stumblingblock before the children of Israel, to eat things sacrificed unto idols, and to commit fornication. 15 So hast thou also them that hold the doctrine of the Nicolaitans, which thing I hate. 16 Repent; or else I will come unto thee quickly, and will fight against them with the sword of my mouth. 17 He that hath an ear, let him hear what the Spirit saith unto the

Visit TimeToFreeAmerica.com/TheHomoDeuce to watch the video clips referenced throughout this book.

churches; To him that overcometh will I give to eat of the hidden manna, and will give him a white stone, and in the stone a new name written, which no man knoweth saving he that receiveth it. 18 And unto the angel of the church in Thyatira write; These things saith the Son of God, who hath his eyes like unto a flame of fire, and his feet are like fine brass; 19 I know thy works, and charity, and service, and faith, and thy patience, and thy works; and the last to be more than the first. 20 Notwithstanding I have a few things against thee, because thou sufferest that woman Jezebel, which calleth herself a prophetess, to teach and to seduce my servants to commit fornication, and to eat things sacrificed unto idols. 21 And I gave her space to repent of her fornication; and she repented not. 22 Behold, I will cast her into a bed, and them that commit adultery with her into great tribulation, except they repent of their deeds. 23 And I will kill her children with death; and all the churches shall know that I am he which searcheth the reins and hearts: and I will give unto every one of you according to your works. 24 But unto you I say, and unto the rest in Thyatira, as many as have not this doctrine, and which have not known the depths of Satan, as they speak; I will put upon you none other burden. 25 But that which ye have already hold fast till I come. 26 And he that overcometh, and keepeth my works unto the end, to him will I give power over the nations: 27 And he shall rule

Visit TimeToFreeAmerica.com/TheHomoDeuce to watch
the video clips referenced throughout this book.

227

them with a rod of iron; as the vessels of a potter shall they be broken to shivers: even as I received of my Father. 28 And I will give him the morning star. 29 He that hath an ear, let him hear what the Spirit saith unto the churches.

CHAPTER 3

1 And unto the angel of the church in Sardis write; These things saith he that hath the seven Spirits of God, and the seven stars; I know thy works, that thou hast a name that thou livest, and art dead. 2 Be watchful, and strengthen the things which remain, that are ready to die: for I have not found thy works perfect before God. 3 Remember therefore how thou hast received and heard, and hold fast, and repent. If therefore thou shalt not watch, I will come on thee as a thief, and thou shalt not know what hour I will come upon thee. 4 Thou hast a few names even in Sardis which have not defiled their garments; and they shall walk with me in white: for they are worthy. 5 He that overcometh, the same shall be clothed in white raiment; and I will not blot out his name out of the book of life, but I will confess his name before my Father, and before his angels. 6 He that hath an ear, let him hear what the Spirit saith unto the churches. 7 And to the angel of the church in Philadelphia write; These things saith he that is holy, he

Visit *TimeToFreeAmerica.com/TheHomoDeuce* to watch the video clips referenced throughout this book.

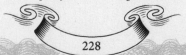

that is true, he that hath the key of David, he that openeth, and no man shutteth; and shutteth, and no man openeth; 8 I know thy works: behold, I have set before thee an open door, and no man can shut it: for thou hast a little strength, and hast kept my word, and hast not denied my name. 9 Behold, I will make them of the synagogue of Satan, which say they are Jews, and are not, but do lie; behold, I will make them to come and worship before thy feet, and to know that I have loved thee. 10 Because thou hast kept the word of my patience, I also will keep thee from the hour of temptation, which shall come upon all the world, to try them that dwell upon the earth. 11 Behold, I come quickly: hold that fast which thou hast, that no man take thy crown. 12 Him that overcometh will I make a pillar in the temple of my God, and he shall go no more out: and I will write upon him the name of my God, and the name of the city of my God, which is new Jerusalem, which cometh down out of heaven from my God: and I will write upon him my new name. 13 He that hath an ear, let him hear what the Spirit saith unto the churches. 14 And unto the angel of the church of the Laodiceans write; These things saith the Amen, the faithful and true witness, the beginning of the creation of God; 15 I know thy works, that thou art neither cold nor hot: I would thou wert cold or hot. 16 So then because thou art lukewarm, and neither cold nor hot, I will spue thee out of my mouth. 17 Because thou sayest, I am

Visit *TimeToFreeAmerica.com/TheHomoDeuce* to watch
the video clips referenced throughout this book.

rich, and increased with goods, and have need of nothing; and knowest not that thou art wretched, and miserable, and poor, and blind, and naked: 18 I counsel thee to buy of me gold tried in the fire, that thou mayest be rich; and white raiment, that thou mayest be clothed, and that the shame of thy nakedness do not appear; and anoint thine eyes with eyesalve, that thou mayest see. 19 As many as I love, I rebuke and chasten: be zealous therefore, and repent. 20 Behold, I stand at the door, and knock: if any man hear my voice, and open the door, I will come in to him, and will sup with him, and he with me. 21 To him that overcometh will I grant to sit with me in my throne, even as I also overcame, and am set down with my Father in his throne. 22 He that hath an ear, let him hear what the Spirit saith unto the churches.

CHAPTER 4

1 After this I looked, and, behold, a door was opened in heaven: and the first voice which I heard was as it were of a trumpet talking with me; which said, Come up hither, and I will shew thee things which must be hereafter. 2 And immediately I was in the spirit: and, behold, a throne was set in heaven, and one sat on the throne. 3 And he that sat was to look upon like a jasper and a sardine stone:

Visit TimeToFreeAmerica.com/TheHomoDeuce to watch the video clips referenced throughout this book.

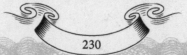

and there was a rainbow round about the throne, in sight like unto an emerald. 4 And round about the throne were four and twenty seats: and upon the seats I saw four and twenty elders sitting, clothed in white raiment; and they had on their heads crowns of gold. 5 And out of the throne proceeded lightnings and thunderings and voices: and there were seven lamps of fire burning before the throne, which are the seven Spirits of God. 6 And before the throne there was a sea of glass like unto crystal: and in the midst of the throne, and round about the throne, were four beasts full of eyes before and behind. 7 And the first beast was like a lion, and the second beast like a calf, and the third beast had a face as a man, and the fourth beast was like a flying eagle. 8 And the four beasts had each of them six wings about him; and they were full of eyes within: and they rest not day and night, saying, Holy, holy, holy, Lord God Almighty, which was, and is, and is to come. 9 And when those beasts give glory and honour and thanks to him that sat on the throne, who liveth for ever and ever, 10 The four and twenty elders fall down before him that sat on the throne, and worship him that liveth for ever and ever, and cast their crowns before the throne, saying, 11 Thou art worthy, O Lord, to receive glory and honour and power: for thou hast created all things, and for thy pleasure they are and were created.

Visit *TimeToFreeAmerica.com/TheHomoDeuce* to watch
the video clips referenced throughout this book.

CHAPTER 5

1 And I saw in the right hand of him that sat on the throne a book written within and on the backside, sealed with seven seals. 2 And I saw a strong angel proclaiming with a loud voice, Who is worthy to open the book, and to loose the seals thereof? 3 And no man in heaven, nor in earth, neither under the earth, was able to open the book, neither to look thereon. 4 And I wept much, because no man was found worthy to open and to read the book, neither to look thereon. 5 And one of the elders saith unto me, Weep not: behold, the Lion of the tribe of Juda, the Root of David, hath prevailed to open the book, and to loose the seven seals thereof. 6 And I beheld, and, lo, in the midst of the throne and of the four beasts, and in the midst of the elders, stood a Lamb as it had been slain, having seven horns and seven eyes, which are the seven Spirits of God sent forth into all the earth. 7 And he came and took the book out of the right hand of him that sat upon the throne. 8 And when he had taken the book, the four beasts and four and twenty elders fell down before the Lamb, having every one of them harps, and golden vials full of odours, which are the prayers of saints. 9 And they sung a new song, saying, Thou art worthy to take the book, and to open the seals thereof: for thou wast slain, and hast

Visit TimeToFreeAmerica.com/TheHomoDeuce to watch the video clips referenced throughout this book.

redeemed us to God by thy blood out of every kindred, and tongue, and people, and nation; 10 And hast made us unto our God kings and priests: and we shall reign on the earth. 11 And I beheld, and I heard the voice of many angels round about the throne and the beasts and the elders: and the number of them was ten thousand times ten thousand, and thousands of thousands; 12 Saying with a loud voice, Worthy is the Lamb that was slain to receive power, and riches, and wisdom, and strength, and honour, and glory, and blessing. 13 And every creature which is in heaven, and on the earth, and under the earth, and such as are in the sea, and all that are in them, heard I saying, Blessing, and honour, and glory, and power, be unto him that sitteth upon the throne, and unto the Lamb for ever and ever. 14 And the four beasts said, Amen. And the four and twenty elders fell down and worshipped him that liveth for ever and ever.

CHAPTER 6

1 And I saw when the Lamb opened one of the seals, and I heard, as it were the noise of thunder, one of the four beasts saying, Come and see. 2 And I saw, and behold a white horse: and he that sat on him had a bow; and a crown was given unto him: and he went forth conquering,

Visit TimeToFreeAmerica.com/TheHomoDeuce to watch
the video clips referenced throughout this book.

and to conquer. 3 And when he had opened the second seal, I heard the second beast say, Come and see. 4 And there went out another horse that was red: and power was given to him that sat thereon to take peace from the earth, and that they should kill one another: and there was given unto him a great sword. 5 And when he had opened the third seal, I heard the third beast say, Come and see. And I beheld, and lo a black horse; and he that sat on him had a pair of balances in his hand. 6 And I heard a voice in the midst of the four beasts say, A measure of wheat for a penny, and three measures of barley for a penny; and see thou hurt not the oil and the wine. 7 And when he had opened the fourth seal, I heard the voice of the fourth beast say, Come and see. 8 And I looked, and behold a pale horse: and his name that sat on him was Death, and Hell followed with him. And power was given unto them over the fourth part of the earth, to kill with sword, and with hunger, and with death, and with the beasts of the earth. 9 And when he had opened the fifth seal, I saw under the altar the souls of them that were slain for the word of God, and for the testimony which they held: 10 And they cried with a loud voice, saying, How long, O Lord, holy and true, dost thou not judge and avenge our blood on them that dwell on the earth? 11 And white robes were given unto every one of them; and it was said unto them, that they should rest yet for a little season, until their fellowservants

Visit TimeToFreeAmerica.com/TheHomoDeuce to watch the video clips referenced throughout this book.

also and their brethren, that should be killed as they were, should be fulfilled. 12 And I beheld when he had opened the sixth seal, and, lo, there was a great earthquake; and the sun became black as sackcloth of hair, and the moon became as blood; 13 And the stars of heaven fell unto the earth, even as a fig tree casteth her untimely figs, when she is shaken of a mighty wind. 14 And the heaven departed as a scroll when it is rolled together; and every mountain and island were moved out of their places. 15 And the kings of the earth, and the great men, and the rich men, and the chief captains, and the mighty men, and every bondman, and every free man, hid themselves in the dens and in the rocks of the mountains; 16 And said to the mountains and rocks, Fall on us, and hide us from the face of him that sitteth on the throne, and from the wrath of the Lamb: 17 For the great day of his wrath is come; and who shall be able to stand?

CHAPTER 7

1 And after these things I saw four angels standing on the four corners of the earth, holding the four winds of the earth, that the wind should not blow on the earth, nor on the sea, nor on any tree. 2 And I saw another angel ascending from the east, having the seal of the living God:

Visit *TimeToFreeAmerica.com/TheHomoDeuce* to watch
the video clips referenced throughout this book.

and he cried with a loud voice to the four angels, to whom it was given to hurt the earth and the sea, 3 Saying, Hurt not the earth, neither the sea, nor the trees, till we have sealed the servants of our God in their foreheads. 4 And I heard the number of them which were sealed: and there were sealed an hundred and forty and four thousand of all the tribes of the children of Israel. 5 Of the tribe of Juda were sealed twelve thousand. Of the tribe of Reuben were sealed twelve thousand. Of the tribe of Gad were sealed twelve thousand. 6 Of the tribe of Aser were sealed twelve thousand. Of the tribe of Nepthalim were sealed twelve thousand. Of the tribe of Manasses were sealed twelve thousand. 7 Of the tribe of Simeon were sealed twelve thousand. Of the tribe of Levi were sealed twelve thousand. Of the tribe of Issachar were sealed twelve thousand. 8 Of the tribe of Zabulon were sealed twelve thousand. Of the tribe of Joseph were sealed twelve thousand. Of the tribe of Benjamin were sealed twelve thousand. 9 After this I beheld, and, lo, a great multitude, which no man could number, of all nations, and kindreds, and people, and tongues, stood before the throne, and before the Lamb, clothed with white robes, and palms in their hands; 10 And cried with a loud voice, saying, Salvation to our God which sitteth upon the throne, and unto the Lamb. 11 And all the angels stood round about the throne, and about the elders and the four beasts, and fell before the throne

Visit TimeToFreeAmerica.com/TheHomoDeuce to watch the video clips referenced throughout this book.

on their faces, and worshipped God, 12 Saying, Amen: Blessing, and glory, and wisdom, and thanksgiving, and honour, and power, and might, be unto our God for ever and ever. Amen. 13 And one of the elders answered, saying unto me, What are these which are arrayed in white robes? and whence came they? 14 And I said unto him, Sir, thou knowest. And he said to me, These are they which came out of great tribulation, and have washed their robes, and made them white in the blood of the Lamb. 15 Therefore are they before the throne of God, and serve him day and night in his temple: and he that sitteth on the throne shall dwell among them. 16 They shall hunger no more, neither thirst any more; neither shall the sun light on them, nor any heat. 17 For the Lamb which is in the midst of the throne shall feed them, and shall lead them unto living fountains of waters: and God shall wipe away all tears from their eyes.

CHAPTER 8

1 And when he had opened the seventh seal, there was silence in heaven about the space of half an hour. 2 And I saw the seven angels which stood before God; and to them were given seven trumpets. 3 And another angel came and stood at the altar, having a golden censer; and there was

Visit TimeToFreeAmerica.com/TheHomoDeuce to watch the video clips referenced throughout this book.

given unto him much incense, that he should offer it with the prayers of all saints upon the golden altar which was before the throne. 4 And the smoke of the incense, which came with the prayers of the saints, ascended up before God out of the angel's hand. 5 And the angel took the censer, and filled it with fire of the altar, and cast it into the earth: and there were voices, and thunderings, and lightnings, and an earthquake. 6 And the seven angels which had the seven trumpets prepared themselves to sound. 7 The first angel sounded, and there followed hail and fire mingled with blood, and they were cast upon the earth: and the third part of trees was burnt up, and all green grass was burnt up. 8 And the second angel sounded, and as it were a great mountain burning with fire was cast into the sea: and the third part of the sea became blood; 9 And the third part of the creatures which were in the sea, and had life, died; and the third part of the ships were destroyed. 10 And the third angel sounded, and there fell a great star from heaven, burning as it were a lamp, and it fell upon the third part of the rivers, and upon the fountains of waters; 11 And the name of the star is called Wormwood: and the third part of the waters became wormwood; and many men died of the waters, because they were made bitter. 12 And the fourth angel sounded, and the third part of the sun was smitten, and the third part of the moon, and the third part of the stars; so as the third part of them was darkened, and the

Visit TimeToFreeAmerica.com/TheHomoDeuce to watch the video clips referenced throughout this book.

day shone not for a third part of it, and the night likewise. 13 And I beheld, and heard an angel flying through the midst of heaven, saying with a loud voice, Woe, woe, woe, to the inhabiters of the earth by reason of the other voices of the trumpet of the three angels, which are yet to sound!

CHAPTER 9

1 And the fifth angel sounded, and I saw a star fall from heaven unto the earth: and to him was given the key of the bottomless pit. 2 And he opened the bottomless pit; and there arose a smoke out of the pit, as the smoke of a great furnace; and the sun and the air were darkened by reason of the smoke of the pit. 3 And there came out of the smoke locusts upon the earth: and unto them was given power, as the scorpions of the earth have power. 4 And it was commanded them that they should not hurt the grass of the earth, neither any green thing, neither any tree; but only those men which have not the seal of God in their foreheads. 5 And to them it was given that they should not kill them, but that they should be tormented five months: and their torment was as the torment of a scorpion, when he striketh a man. 6 And in those days shall men seek death, and shall not find it; and shall desire to die, and death shall flee from them. 7 And the shapes of

Visit TimeToFreeAmerica.com/TheHomoDeuce to watch
the video clips referenced throughout this book.

the locusts were like unto horses prepared unto battle; and on their heads were as it were crowns like gold, and their faces were as the faces of men. 8 And they had hair as the hair of women, and their teeth were as the teeth of lions. 9 And they had breastplates, as it were breastplates of iron; and the sound of their wings was as the sound of chariots of many horses running to battle. 10 And they had tails like unto scorpions, and there were stings in their tails: and their power was to hurt men five months. 11 And they had a king over them, which is the angel of the bottomless pit, whose name in the Hebrew tongue is Abaddon, but in the Greek tongue hath his name Apollyon. 12 One woe is past; and, behold, there come two woes more hereafter. 13 And the sixth angel sounded, and I heard a voice from the four horns of the golden altar which is before God, 14 Saying to the sixth angel which had the trumpet, Loose the four angels which are bound in the great river Euphrates. 15 And the four angels were loosed, which were prepared for an hour, and a day, and a month, and a year, for to slay the third part of men. 16 And the number of the army of the horsemen were two hundred thousand thousand: and I heard the number of them. 17 And thus I saw the horses in the vision, and them that sat on them, having breastplates of fire, and of jacinth, and brimstone: and the heads of the horses were as the heads of lions; and out of their mouths issued fire and smoke and brimstone. 18 By

Visit TimeToFreeAmerica.com/TheHomoDeuce to watch the video clips referenced throughout this book.

these three was the third part of men killed, by the fire, and by the smoke, and by the brimstone, which issued out of their mouths. 19 For their power is in their mouth, and in their tails: for their tails were like unto serpents, and had heads, and with them they do hurt. 20 And the rest of the men which were not killed by these plagues yet repented not of the works of their hands, that they should not worship devils, and idols of gold, and silver, and brass, and stone, and of wood: which neither can see, nor hear, nor walk: 21 Neither repented they of their murders, nor of their sorceries, nor of their fornication, nor of their thefts.

CHAPTER 10

1 And I saw another mighty angel come down from heaven, clothed with a cloud: and a rainbow was upon his head, and his face was as it were the sun, and his feet as pillars of fire: 2 And he had in his hand a little book open: and he set his right foot upon the sea, and his left foot on the earth, 3 And cried with a loud voice, as when a lion roareth: and when he had cried, seven thunders uttered their voices. 4 And when the seven thunders had uttered their voices, I was about to write: and I heard a voice from heaven saying unto me, Seal up those things which the seven thunders uttered, and write them not. 5

Visit TimeToFreeAmerica.com/TheHomoDeuce to watch the video clips referenced throughout this book.

And the angel which I saw stand upon the sea and upon the earth lifted up his hand to heaven, 6 And sware by him that liveth for ever and ever, who created heaven, and the things that therein are, and the earth, and the things that therein are, and the sea, and the things which are therein, that there should be time no longer: 7 But in the days of the voice of the seventh angel, when he shall begin to sound, the mystery of God should be finished, as he hath declared to his servants the prophets. 8 And the voice which I heard from heaven spake unto me again, and said, Go and take the little book which is open in the hand of the angel which standeth upon the sea and upon the earth. 9 And I went unto the angel, and said unto him, Give me the little book. And he said unto me, Take it, and eat it up; and it shall make thy belly bitter, but it shall be in thy mouth sweet as honey. 10 And I took the little book out of the angel's hand, and ate it up; and it was in my mouth sweet as honey: and as soon as I had eaten it, my belly was bitter. 11 And he said unto me, Thou must prophesy again before many peoples, and nations, and tongues, and kings.

CHAPTER 11

1 And there was given me a reed like unto a rod: and the angel stood, saying, Rise, and measure the temple of God,

Visit *TimeToFreeAmerica.com/TheHomoDeuce* to watch
the video clips referenced throughout this book.

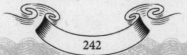

and the altar, and them that worship therein. 2 But the court which is without the temple leave out, and measure it not; for it is given unto the Gentiles: and the holy city shall they tread under foot forty and two months. 3 And I will give power unto my two witnesses, and they shall prophesy a thousand two hundred and threescore days, clothed in sackcloth. 4 These are the two olive trees, and the two candlesticks standing before the God of the earth. 5 And if any man will hurt them, fire proceedeth out of their mouth, and devoureth their enemies: and if any man will hurt them, he must in this manner be killed. 6 These have power to shut heaven, that it rain not in the days of their prophecy: and have power over waters to turn them to blood, and to smite the earth with all plagues, as often as they will. 7 And when they shall have finished their testimony, the beast that ascendeth out of the bottomless pit shall make war against them, and shall overcome them, and kill them. 8 And their dead bodies shall lie in the street of the great city, which spiritually is called Sodom and Egypt, where also our Lord was crucified. 9 And they of the people and kindreds and tongues and nations shall see their dead bodies three days and an half, and shall not suffer their dead bodies to be put in graves. 10 And they that dwell upon the earth shall rejoice over them, and make merry, and shall send gifts one to another; because these two prophets tormented them that dwelt on

Visit TimeToFreeAmerica.com/TheHomoDeuce to watch the video clips referenced throughout this book.

the earth. 11 And after three days and an half the Spirit of life from God entered into them, and they stood upon their feet; and great fear fell upon them which saw them. 12 And they heard a great voice from heaven saying unto them, Come up hither. And they ascended up to heaven in a cloud; and their enemies beheld them. 13 And the same hour was there a great earthquake, and the tenth part of the city fell, and in the earthquake were slain of men seven thousand: and the remnant were affrighted, and gave glory to the God of heaven. 14 The second woe is past; and, behold, the third woe cometh quickly. 15 And the seventh angel sounded; and there were great voices in heaven, saying, The kingdoms of this world are become the kingdoms of our Lord, and of his Christ; and he shall reign for ever and ever. 16 And the four and twenty elders, which sat before God on their seats, fell upon their faces, and worshipped God, 17 Saying, We give thee thanks, O Lord God Almighty, which art, and wast, and art to come; because thou hast taken to thee thy great power, and hast reigned.. 18 And the nations were angry, and thy wrath is come, and the time of the dead, that they should be judged, and that thou shouldest give reward unto thy servants the prophets, and to the saints, and them that fear thy name, small and great; and shouldest destroy them which destroy the earth. 19 And the temple of God was opened in heaven, and there was seen in his temple the ark of his testament:

Visit TimeToFreeAmerica.com/TheHomoDeuce to watch the video clips referenced throughout this book.

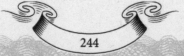

and there were lightnings, and voices, and thunderings, and an earthquake, and great hail.

CHAPTER 12

1 And there appeared a great wonder in heaven; a woman clothed with the sun, and the moon under her feet, and upon her head a crown of twelve stars: 2 And she being with child cried, travailing in birth, and pained to be delivered. 3 And there appeared another wonder in heaven; and behold a great red dragon, having seven heads and ten horns, and seven crowns upon his heads. 4 And his tail drew the third part of the stars of heaven, and did cast them to the earth: and the dragon stood before the woman which was ready to be delivered, for to devour her child as soon as it was born. 5 And she brought forth a man child, who was to rule all nations with a rod of iron: and her child was caught up unto God, and to his throne. 6 And the woman fled into the wilderness, where she hath a place prepared of God, that they should feed her there a thousand two hundred and threescore days. 7 And there was war in heaven: Michael and his angels fought against the dragon; and the dragon fought and his angels, 8 And prevailed not; neither was their place found any more in heaven. 9 And the great dragon was cast out, that old serpent, called the

Visit TimeToFreeAmerica.com/TheHomoDeuce to watch the video clips referenced throughout this book.

Devil, and Satan, which deceiveth the whole world: he was cast out into the earth, and his angels were cast out with him. 10 And I heard a loud voice saying in heaven, Now is come salvation, and strength, and the kingdom of our God, and the power of his Christ: for the accuser of our brethren is cast down, which accused them before our God day and night. 11 And they overcame him by the blood of the Lamb, and by the word of their testimony; and they loved not their lives unto the death. 12 Therefore rejoice, ye heavens, and ye that dwell in them. Woe to the inhabiters of the earth and of the sea! for the devil is come down unto you, having great wrath, because he knoweth that he hath but a short time. 13 And when the dragon saw that he was cast unto the earth, he persecuted the woman which brought forth the man child. 14 And to the woman were given two wings of a great eagle, that she might fly into the wilderness, into her place, where she is nourished for a time, and times, and half a time, from the face of the serpent. 15 And the serpent cast out of his mouth water as a flood after the woman, that he might cause her to be carried away of the flood. 16 And the earth helped the woman, and the earth opened her mouth, and swallowed up the flood which the dragon cast out of his mouth. 17 And the dragon was wroth with the woman, and went to make war with the remnant of her seed, which keep the commandments of God, and have the testimony of Jesus Christ.

Visit *TimeToFreeAmerica.com/TheHomoDeuce* to watch
the video clips referenced throughout this book.

CHAPTER 13

1 And I stood upon the sand of the sea, and saw a beast rise up out of the sea, having seven heads and ten horns, and upon his horns ten crowns, and upon his heads the name of blasphemy. 2 And the beast which I saw was like unto a leopard, and his feet were as the feet of a bear, and his mouth as the mouth of a lion: and the dragon gave him his power, and his seat, and great authority. 3 And I saw one of his heads as it were wounded to death; and his deadly wound was healed: and all the world wondered after the beast. 4 And they worshipped the dragon which gave power unto the beast: and they worshipped the beast, saying, Who is like unto the beast? who is able to make war with him? 5 And there was given unto him a mouth speaking great things and blasphemies; and power was given unto him to continue forty and two months. 6 And he opened his mouth in blasphemy against God, to blaspheme his name, and his tabernacle, and them that dwell in heaven. 7 And it was given unto him to make war with the saints, and to overcome them: and power was given him over all kindreds, and tongues, and nations. 8 And all that dwell upon the earth shall worship him, whose names are not written in the book of life of the Lamb slain from the foundation of the world. 9 If any man have an

*Visit TimeToFreeAmerica.com/TheHomoDeuce to watch
the video clips referenced throughout this book.*

ear, let him hear. 10 He that leadeth into captivity shall go into captivity: he that killeth with the sword must be killed with the sword. Here is the patience and the faith of the saints. 11 And I beheld another beast coming up out of the earth; and he had two horns like a lamb, and he spake as a dragon. 12 And he exerciseth all the power of the first beast before him, and causeth the earth and them which dwell therein to worship the first beast, whose deadly wound was healed. 13 And he doeth great wonders, so that he maketh fire come down from heaven on the earth in the sight of men, 14 And deceiveth them that dwell on the earth by the means of those miracles which he had power to do in the sight of the beast; saying to them that dwell on the earth, that they should make an image to the beast, which had the wound by a sword, and did live. 15 And he had power to give life unto the image of the beast, that the image of the beast should both speak, and cause that as many as would not worship the image of the beast should be killed. 16 And he causeth all, both small and great, rich and poor, free and bond, to receive a mark in their right hand, or in their foreheads: 17 And that no man might buy or sell, save he that had the mark, or the name of the beast, or the number of his name. 18 Here is wisdom. Let him that hath understanding count the number of the beast: for it is the number of a man; and his number is Six hundred threescore and six.

Visit TimeToFreeAmerica.com/TheHomoDeuce to watch the video clips referenced throughout this book.

CHAPTER 14

1 And I looked, and, lo, a Lamb stood on the mount Sion, and with him an hundred forty and four thousand, having his Father's name written in their foreheads. 2 And I heard a voice from heaven, as the voice of many waters, and as the voice of a great thunder: and I heard the voice of harpers harping with their harps: 3 And they sung as it were a new song before the throne, and before the four beasts, and the elders: and no man could learn that song but the hundred and forty and four thousand, which were redeemed from the earth. 4 These are they which were not defiled with women; for they are virgins. These are they which follow the Lamb whithersoever he goeth. These were redeemed from among men, being the firstfruits unto God and to the Lamb. 5 And in their mouth was found no guile: for they are without fault before the throne of God. 6 And I saw another angel fly in the midst of heaven, having the everlasting gospel to preach unto them that dwell on the earth, and to every nation, and kindred, and tongue, and people, 7 Saying with a loud voice, Fear God, and give glory to him; for the hour of his judgment is come: and worship him that made heaven, and earth, and the sea, and the fountains of waters. 8 And there followed another angel, saying, Babylon is fallen, is fallen, that great city,

Visit TimeToFreeAmerica.com/TheHomoDeuce to watch the video clips referenced throughout this book.

because she made all nations drink of the wine of the wrath of her fornication. 9 And the third angel followed them, saying with a loud voice, If any man worship the beast and his image, and receive his mark in his forehead, or in his hand, 10 The same shall drink of the wine of the wrath of God, which is poured out without mixture into the cup of his indignation; and he shall be tormented with fire and brimstone in the presence of the holy angels, and in the presence of the Lamb: 11 And the smoke of their torment ascendeth up for ever and ever: and they have no rest day nor night, who worship the beast and his image, and whosoever receiveth the mark of his name. 12 Here is the patience of the saints: here are they that keep the commandments of God, and the faith of Jesus. 13 And I heard a voice from heaven saying unto me, Write, Blessed are the dead which die in the Lord from henceforth: Yea, saith the Spirit, that they may rest from their labours; and their works do follow them. 14 And I looked, and behold a white cloud, and upon the cloud one sat like unto the Son of man, having on his head a golden crown, and in his hand a sharp sickle. 15 And another angel came out of the temple, crying with a loud voice to him that sat on the cloud, Thrust in thy sickle, and reap: for the time is come for thee to reap; for the harvest of the earth is ripe. 16 And he that sat on the cloud thrust in his sickle on the earth; and the earth was reaped. 17 And another angel came out

Visit TimeToFreeAmerica.com/TheHomoDeuce to watch the video clips referenced throughout this book.

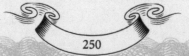

of the temple which is in heaven, he also having a sharp sickle. 18 And another angel came out from the altar, which had power over fire; and cried with a loud cry to him that had the sharp sickle, saying, Thrust in thy sharp sickle, and gather the clusters of the vine of the earth; for her grapes are fully ripe. 19 And the angel thrust in his sickle into the earth, and gathered the vine of the earth, and cast it into the great winepress of the wrath of God. 20 And the winepress was trodden without the city, and blood came out of the winepress, even unto the horse bridles, by the space of a thousand and six hundred furlongs.

CHAPTER 15

1 And I saw another sign in heaven, great and marvellous, seven angels having the seven last plagues; for in them is filled up the wrath of God. 2 And I saw as it were a sea of glass mingled with fire: and them that had gotten the victory over the beast, and over his image, and over his mark, and over the number of his name, stand on the sea of glass, having the harps of God. 3 And they sing the song of Moses the servant of God, and the song of the Lamb, saying, Great and marvellous are thy works, Lord God Almighty; just and true are thy ways, thou King of saints. 4 Who shall not fear thee, O Lord, and glorify thy

Visit TimeToFreeAmerica.com/TheHomoDeuce to watch the video clips referenced throughout this book.

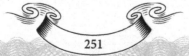

name? for thou only art holy: for all nations shall come and worship before thee; for thy judgments are made manifest. 5 And after that I looked, and, behold, the temple of the tabernacle of the testimony in heaven was opened:

CHAPTER 16

1 And I heard a great voice out of the temple saying to the seven angels, Go your ways, and pour out the vials of the wrath of God upon the earth. 2 And the first went, and poured out his vial upon the earth; and there fell a noisome and grievous sore upon the men which had the mark of the beast, and upon them which worshipped his image. 3 And the second angel poured out his vial upon the sea; and it became as the blood of a dead man: and every living soul died in the sea. 4 And the third angel poured out his vial upon the rivers and fountains of waters; and they became blood. 5 And I heard the angel of the waters say, Thou art righteous, O Lord, which art, and wast, and shalt be, because thou hast judged thus. 6 For they have shed the blood of saints and prophets, and thou hast given them blood to drink; for they are worthy. 7 And I heard another out of the altar say, Even so, Lord God Almighty, true and righteous are thy judgments. 8 And the fourth angel poured out his vial upon the sun; and power was given unto him to

Visit TimeToFreeAmerica.com/TheHomoDeuce to watch
the video clips referenced throughout this book.

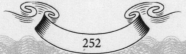

scorch men with fire. 9 And men were scorched with great heat, and blasphemed the name of God, which hath power over these plagues: and they repented not to give him glory. 10 And the fifth angel poured out his vial upon the seat of the beast; and his kingdom was full of darkness; and they gnawed their tongues for pain, 11 And blasphemed the God of heaven because of their pains and their sores, and repented not of their deeds. 12 And the sixth angel poured out his vial upon the great river Euphrates; and the water thereof was dried up, that the way of the kings of the east might be prepared. 13 And I saw three unclean spirits like frogs come out of the mouth of the dragon, and out of the mouth of the beast, and out of the mouth of the false prophet. 14 For they are the spirits of devils, working miracles, which go forth unto the kings of the earth and of the whole world, to gather them to the battle of that great day of God Almighty. 15 Behold, I come as a thief. Blessed is he that watcheth, and keepeth his garments, lest he walk naked, and they see his shame. 16 And he gathered them together into a place called in the Hebrew tongue Armageddon. 17 And the seventh angel poured out his vial into the air; and there came a great voice out of the temple of heaven, from the throne, saying, It is done. 18 And there were voices, and thunders, and lightnings; and there was a great earthquake, such as was not since men were upon the earth, so mighty an earthquake, and so great. 19 And

*Visit TimeToFreeAmerica.com/TheHomoDeuce to watch
the video clips referenced throughout this book.*

the great city was divided into three parts, and the cities of the nations fell: and great Babylon came in remembrance before God, to give unto her the cup of the wine of the fierceness of his wrath. 20 And every island fled away, and the mountains were not found. 21 And there fell upon men a great hail out of heaven, every stone about the weight of a talent: and men blasphemed God because of the plague of the hail; for the plague thereof was exceeding great.

CHAPTER 17

1 And there came one of the seven angels which had the seven vials, and talked with me, saying unto me, Come hither; I will shew unto thee the judgment of the great whore that sitteth upon many waters: 2 With whom the kings of the earth have committed fornication, and the inhabitants of the earth have been made drunk with the wine of her fornication. 3 So he carried me away in the spirit into the wilderness: and I saw a woman sit upon a scarlet coloured beast, full of names of blasphemy, having seven heads and ten horns. 4 And the woman was arrayed in purple and scarlet colour, and decked with gold and precious stones and pearls, having a golden cup in her hand full of abominations and filthiness of her fornication: 5 And upon her forehead was a name written, MYSTERY,

Visit TimeToFreeAmerica.com/TheHomoDeuce to watch
the video clips referenced throughout this book.

BABYLON THE GREAT, THE MOTHER OF HARLOTS AND ABOMINATIONS OF THE EARTH. 6 And I saw the woman drunken with the blood of the saints, and with the blood of the martyrs of Jesus: and when I saw her, I wondered with great admiration. 7 And the angel said unto me, Wherefore didst thou marvel? I will tell thee the mystery of the woman, and of the beast that carrieth her, which hath the seven heads and ten horns. 8 The beast that thou sawest was, and is not; and shall ascend out of the bottomless pit, and go into perdition: and they that dwell on the earth shall wonder, whose names were not written in the book of life from the foundation of the world, when they behold the beast that was, and is not, and yet is. 9 And here is the mind which hath wisdom. The seven heads are seven mountains, on which the woman sitteth. 10 And there are seven kings: five are fallen, and one is, and the other is not yet come; and when he cometh, he must continue a short space. 11 And the beast that was, and is not, even he is the eighth, and is of the seven, and goeth into perdition. 12 And the ten horns which thou sawest are ten kings, which have received no kingdom as yet; but receive power as kings one hour with the beast. 13 These have one mind, and shall give their power and strength unto the beast. 14 These shall make war with the Lamb, and the Lamb shall overcome them: for he is Lord of lords, and King of kings: and they that are with him are called, and

Visit *TimeToFreeAmerica.com/TheHomoDeuce* to watch
the video clips referenced throughout this book.

chosen, and faithful. 15 And he saith unto me, The waters which thou sawest, where the whore sitteth, are peoples, and multitudes, and nations, and tongues. 16 And the ten horns which thou sawest upon the beast, these shall hate the whore, and shall make her desolate and naked, and shall eat her flesh, and burn her with fire. 17 For God hath put in their hearts to fulfil his will, and to agree, and give their kingdom unto the beast, until the words of God shall be fulfilled. 18 And the woman which thou sawest is that great city, which reigneth over the kings of the earth.

CHAPTER 18

1 And after these things I saw another angel come down from heaven, having great power; and the earth was lightened with his glory. 2 And he cried mightily with a strong voice, saying, Babylon the great is fallen, is fallen, and is become the habitation of devils, and the hold of every foul spirit, and a cage of every unclean and hateful bird. 3 For all nations have drunk of the wine of the wrath of her fornication, and the kings of the earth have committed fornication with her, and the merchants of the earth are waxed rich through the abundance of her delicacies. 4 And I heard another voice from heaven, saying, Come out of her, my people, that ye be not partakers of her sins, and that

Visit TimeToFreeAmerica.com/TheHomoDeuce to watch
the video clips referenced throughout this book.

ye receive not of her plagues. 5 For her sins have reached unto heaven, and God hath remembered her iniquities. 6 Reward her even as she rewarded you, and double unto her double according to her works: in the cup which she hath filled fill to her double. 7 How much she hath glorified herself, and lived deliciously, so much torment and sorrow give her: for she saith in her heart, I sit a queen, and am no widow, and shall see no sorrow. 8 Therefore shall her plagues come in one day, death, and mourning, and famine; and she shall be utterly burned with fire: for strong is the Lord God who judgeth her. 9 And the kings of the earth, who have committed fornication and lived deliciously with her, shall bewail her, and lament for her, when they shall see the smoke of her burning, 10 Standing afar off for the fear of her torment, saying, Alas, alas, that great city Babylon, that mighty city! for in one hour is thy judgment come. 11 And the merchants of the earth shall weep and mourn over her; for no man buyeth their merchandise any more: 12 The merchandise of gold, and silver, and precious stones, and of pearls, and fine linen, and purple, and silk, and scarlet, and all thyine wood, and all manner vessels of ivory, and all manner vessels of most precious wood, and of brass, and iron, and marble, 13 And cinnamon, and odours, and ointments, and frankincense, and wine, and oil, and fine flour, and wheat, and beasts, and sheep, and horses, and chariots, and slaves, and souls

Visit *TimeToFreeAmerica.com/TheHomoDeuce* to watch
the video clips referenced throughout this book.

of men. 14 And the fruits that thy soul lusted after are departed from thee, and all things which were dainty and goodly are departed from thee, and thou shalt find them no more at all. 15 The merchants of these things, which were made rich by her, shall stand afar off for the fear of her torment, weeping and wailing, 16 And saying, Alas, alas, that great city, that was clothed in fine linen, and purple, and scarlet, and decked with gold, and precious stones, and pearls! 17 For in one hour so great riches is come to nought. And every shipmaster, and all the company in ships, and sailors, and as many as trade by sea, stood afar off, 18 And cried when they saw the smoke of her burning, saying, What city is like unto this great city! 19 And they cast dust on their heads, and cried, weeping and wailing, saying, Alas, alas, that great city, wherein were made rich all that had ships in the sea by reason of her costliness! for in one hour is she made desolate. 20 Rejoice over her, thou heaven, and ye holy apostles and prophets; for God hath avenged you on her. 21 And a mighty angel took up a stone like a great millstone, and cast it into the sea, saying, Thus with violence shall that great city Babylon be thrown down, and shall be found no more at all. 22 And the voice of harpers, and musicians, and of pipers, and trumpeters, shall be heard no more at all in thee; and no craftsman, of whatsoever craft he be, shall be found any more in thee; and the sound of a millstone shall be heard no more at all

Visit TimeToFreeAmerica.com/TheHomoDeuce to watch the video clips referenced throughout this book.

in thee; 23 And the light of a candle shall shine no more at all in thee; and the voice of the bridegroom and of the bride shall be heard no more at all in thee: for thy merchants were the great men of the earth; for by thy sorceries were all nations deceived. 24 And in her was found the blood of prophets, and of saints, and of all that were slain upon the earth.

CHAPTER 19

1 And after these things I heard a great voice of much people in heaven, saying, Alleluia; Salvation, and glory, and honour, and power, unto the Lord our God: 2 For true and righteous are his judgments: for he hath judged the great whore, which did corrupt the earth with her fornication, and hath avenged the blood of his servants at her hand. 3 And again they said, Alleluia. And her smoke rose up for ever and ever. 4 And the four and twenty elders and the four beasts fell down and worshipped God that sat on the throne, saying, Amen; Alleluia. 5 And a voice came out of the throne, saying, Praise our God, all ye his servants, and ye that fear him, both small and great. 6 And I heard as it were the voice of a great multitude, and as the voice of many waters, and as the voice of mighty thunderings, saying, Alleluia: for the Lord God omnipotent reigneth.

Visit TimeToFreeAmerica.com/TheHomoDeuce to watch the video clips referenced throughout this book.

7 Let us be glad and rejoice, and give honour to him: for the marriage of the Lamb is come, and his wife hath made herself ready. 8 And to her was granted that she should be arrayed in fine linen, clean and white: for the fine linen is the righteousness of saints. 9 And he saith unto me, Write, Blessed are they which are called unto the marriage supper of the Lamb. And he saith unto me, These are the true sayings of God. 10 And I fell at his feet to worship him. And he said unto me, See thou do it not: I am thy fellowservant, and of thy brethren that have the testimony of Jesus: worship God: for the testimony of Jesus is the spirit of prophecy. 11 And I saw heaven opened, and behold a white horse; and he that sat upon him was called Faithful and True, and in righteousness he doth judge and make war. 12 His eyes were as a flame of fire, and on his head were many crowns; and he had a name written, that no man knew, but he himself. 13 And he was clothed with a vesture dipped in blood: and his name is called The Word of God. 14 And the armies which were in heaven followed him upon white horses, clothed in fine linen, white and clean. 15 And out of his mouth goeth a sharp sword, that with it he should smite the nations: and he shall rule them with a rod of iron: and he treadeth the winepress of the fierceness and wrath of Almighty God. 16 And he hath on his vesture and on his thigh a name written, KING OF KINGS, AND LORD OF LORDS. 17 And I saw an angel standing in the sun; and

Visit TimeToFreeAmerica.com/TheHomoDeuce to watch the video clips referenced throughout this book.

he cried with a loud voice, saying to all the fowls that fly in the midst of heaven, Come and gather yourselves together unto the supper of the great God; 18 That ye may eat the flesh of kings, and the flesh of captains, and the flesh of mighty men, and the flesh of horses, and of them that sit on them, and the flesh of all men, both free and bond, both small and great. 19 And I saw the beast, and the kings of the earth, and their armies, gathered together to make war against him that sat on the horse, and against his army. 20 And the beast was taken, and with him the false prophet that wrought miracles before him, with which he deceived them that had received the mark of the beast, and them that worshipped his image. These both were cast alive into a lake of fire burning with brimstone. 21 And the remnant were slain with the sword of him that sat upon the horse, which sword proceeded out of his mouth: and all the fowls were filled with their flesh.

CHAPTER 20

1 And I saw an angel come down from heaven, having the key of the bottomless pit and a great chain in his hand. 2 And he laid hold on the dragon, that old serpent, which is the Devil, and Satan, and bound him a thousand years, 3 And cast him into the bottomless pit, and shut him up,

Visit TimeToFreeAmerica.com/TheHomoDeuce to watch the video clips referenced throughout this book.

and set a seal upon him, that he should deceive the nations no more, till the thousand years should be fulfilled: and after that he must be loosed a little season. 4 And I saw thrones, and they sat upon them, and judgment was given unto them: and I saw the souls of them that were beheaded for the witness of Jesus, and for the word of God, and which had not worshipped the beast, neither his image, neither had received his mark upon their foreheads, or in their hands; and they lived and reigned with Christ a thousand years. 5 But the rest of the dead lived not again until the thousand years were finished. This is the first resurrection. 6 Blessed and holy is he that hath part in the first resurrection: on such the second death hath no power, but they shall be priests of God and of Christ, and shall reign with him a thousand years. 7 And when the thousand years are expired, Satan shall be loosed out of his prison, 8 And shall go out to deceive the nations which are in the four quarters of the earth, Gog and Magog, to gather them together to battle: the number of whom is as the sand of the sea. 9 And they went up on the breadth of the earth, and compassed the camp of the saints about, and the beloved city: and fire came down from God out of heaven, and devoured them. 10 And the devil that deceived them was cast into the lake of fire and brimstone, where the beast and the false prophet are, and shall be tormented day and night for ever and ever. 11 And I saw a great white throne,

Visit TimeToFreeAmerica.com/TheHomoDeuce to watch the video clips referenced throughout this book.

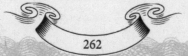

and him that sat on it, from whose face the earth and the heaven fled away; and there was found no place for them. 12 And I saw the dead, small and great, stand before God; and the books were opened: and another book was opened, which is the book of life: and the dead were judged out of those things which were written in the books, according to their works. 13 And the sea gave up the dead which were in it; and death and hell delivered up the dead which were in them: and they were judged every man according to their works. 14 And death and hell were cast into the lake of fire. This is the second death. 15 And whosoever was not found written in the book of life was cast into the lake of fire.

CHAPTER 21

1 And I saw a new heaven and a new earth: for the first heaven and the first earth were passed away; and there was no more sea. 2 And I John saw the holy city, new Jerusalem, coming down from God out of heaven, prepared as a bride adorned for her husband. 3 And I heard a great voice out of heaven saying, Behold, the tabernacle of God is with men, and he will dwell with them, and they shall be his people, and God himself shall be with them, and be their God. 4 And God shall wipe away all tears from their eyes; and there shall be no more death, neither sorrow, nor

Visit TimeToFreeAmerica.com/TheHomoDeuce to watch the video clips referenced throughout this book.

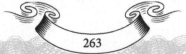

crying, neither shall there be any more pain: for the former things are passed away. 5 And he that sat upon the throne said, Behold, I make all things new. And he said unto me, Write: for these words are true and faithful. 6 And he said unto me, It is done. I am Alpha and Omega, the beginning and the end. I will give unto him that is athirst of the fountain of the water of life freely. 7 He that overcometh shall inherit all things; and I will be his God, and he shall be my son. 8 But the fearful, and unbelieving, and the abominable, and murderers, and whoremongers, and sorcerers, and idolaters, and all liars, shall have their part in the lake which burneth with fire and brimstone: which is the second death. 9 And there came unto me one of the seven angels which had the seven vials full of the seven last plagues, and talked with me, saying, Come hither, I will shew thee the bride, the Lamb's wife. 10 And he carried me away in the spirit to a great and high mountain, and shewed me that great city, the holy Jerusalem, descending out of heaven from God, 11 Having the glory of God: and her light was like unto a stone most precious, even like a jasper stone, clear as crystal; 12 And had a wall great and high, and had twelve gates, and at the gates twelve angels, and names written thereon, which are the names of the twelve tribes of the children of Israel: 13 On the east three gates; on the north three gates; on the south three gates; and on the west three gates. 14 And the wall of the city had

Visit TimeToFreeAmerica.com/TheHomoDeuce to watch the video clips referenced throughout this book.

twelve foundations, and in them the names of the twelve apostles of the Lamb. 15 And he that talked with me had a golden reed to measure the city, and the gates thereof, and the wall thereof. 16 And the city lieth foursquare, and the length is as large as the breadth: and he measured the city with the reed, twelve thousand furlongs. The length and the breadth and the height of it are equal. 17 And he measured the wall thereof, an hundred and forty and four cubits, according to the measure of a man, that is, of the angel. 18 And the building of the wall of it was of jasper: and the city was pure gold, like unto clear glass. 19 And the foundations of the wall of the city were garnished with all manner of precious stones. The first foundation was jasper; the second, sapphire; the third, a chalcedony; the fourth, an emerald; 20 The fifth, sardonyx; the sixth, sardius; the seventh, chrysolite; the eighth, beryl; the ninth, a topaz; the tenth, a chrysoprasus; the eleventh, a jacinth; the twelfth, an amethyst. 21 And the twelve gates were twelve pearls; every several gate was of one pearl: and the street of the city was pure gold, as it were transparent glass. 22 And I saw no temple therein: for the Lord God Almighty and the Lamb are the temple of it. 23 And the city had no need of the sun, neither of the moon, to shine in it: for the glory of God did lighten it, and the Lamb is the light thereof. 24 And the nations of them which are saved shall walk in the light of it: and the kings of the earth

Visit TimeToFreeAmerica.com/TheHomoDeuce to watch
the video clips referenced throughout this book.

do bring their glory and honour into it. 25 And the gates of it shall not be shut at all by day: for there shall be no night there. 26 And they shall bring the glory and honour of the nations into it. 27 And there shall in no wise enter into it any thing that defileth, neither whatsoever worketh abomination, or maketh a lie: but they which are written in the Lamb's book of life.

CHAPTER 22

1 And he shewed me a pure river of water of life, clear as crystal, proceeding out of the throne of God and of the Lamb. 2 In the midst of the street of it, and on either side of the river, was there the tree of life, which bare twelve manner of fruits, and yielded her fruit every month: and the leaves of the tree were for the healing of the nations. 3 And there shall be no more curse: but the throne of God and of the Lamb shall be in it; and his servants shall serve him: 4 And they shall see his face; and his name shall be in their foreheads. 5 And there shall be no night there; and they need no candle, neither light of the sun; for the Lord God giveth them light: and they shall reign for ever and ever. 6 And he said unto me, These sayings are faithful and true: and the Lord God of the holy prophets sent his angel to shew unto his servants the things which must shortly be

Visit TimeToFreeAmerica.com/TheHomoDeuce to watch the video clips referenced throughout this book.

done. 7 Behold, I come quickly: blessed is he that keepeth the sayings of the prophecy of this book. 8 And I John saw these things, and heard them. And when I had heard and seen, I fell down to worship before the feet of the angel which shewed me these things. 9 Then saith he unto me, See thou do it not: for I am thy fellowservant, and of thy brethren the prophets, and of them which keep the sayings of this book: worship God. 10 And he saith unto me, Seal not the sayings of the prophecy of this book: for the time is at hand. 11 He that is unjust, let him be unjust still: and he which is filthy, let him be filthy still: and he that is righteous, let him be righteous still: and he that is holy, let him be holy still. 12 And, behold, I come quickly; and my reward is with me, to give every man according as his work shall be. 13 I am Alpha and Omega, the beginning and the end, the first and the last. 14 Blessed are they that do his commandments, that they may have right to the tree of life, and may enter in through the gates into the city. 15 For without are dogs, and sorcerers, and whoremongers, and murderers, and idolaters, and whosoever loveth and maketh a lie. 16 I Jesus have sent mine angel to testify unto you these things in the churches. I am the root and the offspring of David, and the bright and morning star. 17 And the Spirit and the bride say, Come. And let him that heareth say, Come. And let him that is athirst come. And whosoever will, let him take the water of life freely.

Visit TimeToFreeAmerica.com/TheHomoDeuce to watch
the video clips referenced throughout this book.

18 For I testify unto every man that heareth the words of the prophecy of this book, If any man shall add unto these things, God shall add unto him the plagues that are written in this book: 19 And if any man shall take away from the words of the book of this prophecy, God shall take away his part out of the book of life, and out of the holy city, and from the things which are written in this book. 20 He which testifieth these things saith, Surely I come quickly. Amen. Even so, come, Lord Jesus. 21 The grace of our Lord Jesus Christ be with you all. Amen.

Visit TimeToFreeAmerica.com/TheHomoDeuce to watch the video clips referenced throughout this book.

ACTION ITEMS

1. Pass on what you've learned by writing a Google Review. search for "ThriveTime Show Jenks" on Google Maps and write a review today!

2. Don't miss a radio show or podcast. Subscribe on Itunes, Spotify, Stitcher or listen at ThrivetimeShow.com

3. Get all of the interactive downloadables by signing up today at ThriveTimeShow.com.

WANT MORE?

Check out the Ultimate Textbook for Starting, Running & Growing Your Own Business!

Start Here

NEVER before has entrepreneurship been delivered in an UNFILTERED, real and raw way... until now. This book is NOT for people that want a politically correct and silver-lined happy-go-lucky view of entrepreneurship. That's crap. Supported by case studies and testimonials from entrepreneurs that have grown their businesses all over the planet using these best practice systems, former U.S. Small Business Administration Entrepreneur of the Year, Clay Clark, shares the specific action steps for successful business systems, hilarious stories from situations that every entrepreneur faces, and entrepreneurship factoids that are guaranteed to blow your mind.

Invite a Friend to Join You at the World's Best 2-Day Intensive Business Workshop

Get specific and practical training on how to grow your business

www.ThriveTimeShow.com/Conference

WANT ONE-ON-ONE MENTORSHIP AND BUSINESS COACHING? VISIT WWW.THRIVETIMESHOW.COM/COACHING

Let our team help you execute your action items and guide you down the proven path (see ThriveTimeShow.com)

WANT TO KNOW EVEN MORE?

CHECK OUT ALL OF CLAY'S BOOKS

START HERE
The World's Best Business Growth & Consulting Book: Business Growth Strategies from the World's Best Business Coach.

DON'T LET YOUR EMPLOYEES HOLD YOU HOSTAGE
This candid book shares how to avoid being held hostage by employees.

MAKE YOUR LIFE EPIC
Clay shares his journey and struggle from the dorm room to the board room during his raw and action-packed story of how he built DJConnection.com.

THE ENTREPRENEUR'S DRAGON ENERGY
The Mindset Kanye, Trump and You Need to Succeed.

BOOM
The 14 Proven Steps to Business Success.

F6 JOURNAL
Meta Thrive Time Journal.

JACKASSARY
Jackassery will serve as a beacon of light for other entrepreneurs that are looking to avoid troublesome employees and difficult situations. This is real. This is raw. This is unfiltered entrepreneurship.

THE ART OF GETTING THINGS DONE
Clay Clark breaks down the proven, time-tested and time freedom creating super moves that you can use to create both the time freedom and financial freedom that most people only dream about.

HOW TO REPEL FRIENDS AND NOT INFLUENCE PEOPLE
The epic whale of a tale featuring America's self proclaimed most humble male.

THRIVE
How to Take Control of Your Destiny and Move Beyond Surviving... Now!

SEARCH ENGINE DOMINATION
Learn the Proven System We've Used to Earn Millions.

SALES DOMINATION
Clay Clark is a master of selling and now he wants to teach you his proven processes, scalable systems and sales mastery moves in a humorous and practical way.

WHEEL OF WEALTH
An Entrepreneur's Action Guide.

WILL NOT WORK FOR FOOD
9 Big Ideas for Effectively Managing Your Business in an Increasingly Dumb, Distracted & Dishonest America.

TRADE-UPS
Learn how to design and live the life you love, how to find and create the time needed to get things done in a world filled with endless digital distractions, and more!

IF MY WALLS COULD TALK
The Notes, Quotes, & Epiphanies I've Written On Clay's Office Walls. (Hardcover).

IT'S NOT LONELY AT THE TOP
15 Keys to achieving a successful, peaceful, and drama-free life. (3/4 of this book is handwritten by Clay Clark, himself).

PODCAST DOMINATION 101
This book will show you how to prepare, record, launch, and begin generating income from your podcast, all from your home studio!

ENTREPRENEURSHIP: SIMPLIFIED, AMPLIFIED, & VISUALIZED
Throughout my career, I have been blessed to achieve tremendous success both as an entrepreneur and as a podcast host.

FEAR UNMASKED
Fear Unmasked gives you the essential information you need to know about the coronavirus, the government shutdown, and the media that is perpetuating the hysteria.

FEAR UNMASKED 2.0
Updated and revised for 2021. Fear Unmasked 2.0 provides more resources to kill the spirit of fear and giving YOU an action plan to save America.

THE GREAT RESET VERSUS THE GREAT AWAKENING
The Great Reset Versus The Great Awakening breaks down this EPIC battle between good and evil.